Dangerous Classes

This book provides an authoritative and much needed critical review of British and American debates about the underclass, set in the context of both historical equivalents and policy issues. The idea of an underclass is based on a notion of social exclusion, be it cultural or structural in nature. It strikes a contrast with the idea of social citizenship, a condition notionally guaranteed by welfare rights. In accepted definitions of the underclass, state dependence has come to be seen as a badge of exclusion rather than a guarantee of inclusion. There has been a gradual shift of emphasis in recent commentary from concern with social rights to anxiety about social obligations, often relating to the enforcement of the work ethic. Implicit in much of the literature is an inconclusive examination of gender roles, and particularly the failure of single mothers to fulfil their social duties. The ambiguities and contradictions of this position are uncovered. So too is the neglected issue of migrant labour and its use as a source of labour on terms not acceptable to the native population. The implications of this phenomenon for questions of social inclusion and the definition of the underclass are then considered in the wider context of the social construction of the labour market.

The book has emerged from the author's longstanding interest and research in unemployment, labour market change, gender relations and social policy. It will be of interest to students and researchers in all of these fields.

Lydia Morris is Senior Lecturer in Sociology at the University of Essex.

Dangerous Classes

The Underclass and Social Citizenship

Lydia Morris

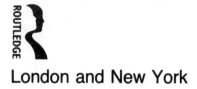

London and New York

First published 1994
by Routledge
11 New Fetter Lane, London EC4P 4EE

Simultaneously published in the USA and Canada
by Routledge
29 West 35th Street, New York, NY 10001

Typeset in Times by J&L Composition Ltd, Filey, North Yorkshire
Printed and bound in Great Britain by
Biddles Ltd, Guildford and King's Lynn

British Library Cataloguing in Publication Data
A catalogue record for this book is available from the British Library

Library of Congress Cataloging in Publication Data
Morris, Lydia, 1949–
    Dangerous classes: the underclass and social citizenship / Lydia
Morris.
        p.   cm.
    Includes bibliographical references and index.
    ISBN 0–415–05013–8: $45.00.—ISBN 0–415–05014–6: $14.95
    1. Marginality, Social—United States.   2. Marginality, Social—
Great Britain.   3. United States—Social conditions—1980–.
4. Great Britain—Social conditions—1980–.   5. Poor—United States.
6. Poor—Great Britain.   I. Title.
HN90.M26M67   1993   93–24569
305.5′6—dc20   CIP

ISBN 0–415–05013–8 (hbk)
        0–415–05014–6 (pbk)

Contents

Many thanks to Irving Velody who gave me the title with all its ambiguity

Introduction

In the course of the 1980s, both Britain and America have seen two taken-for-granted features of social life come under challenge. The social organisation of both countries has been built around full time paid employment in a capitalist system of production, with a specific role for the nuclear family household through the daily and generational reproduction of the workforce. This arrangement is predicated upon a gendered division of labour in which the man is the principal earner and the woman has the main responsibility for domestic life, and it has not, so far, been fundamentally altered by the entry of a majority of married women into the labour force (Morris, 1990). The last decade has, however, seen high and enduring levels of male unemployment as well as an increase in the proportion of single mother households. Whether these two phenomena are related is not entirely clear, but in combination they certainly give cause to doubt the stability of key social institutions.

Two types of problem emerge for the sociologist. The first concerns explanation and interpretation: why have the changes come about and what will they mean for the future organisation of society? The second concerns the models which sociologists have constructed for understanding the social world: are they themselves time-bound and inadequate to accommodate change? One response which has promised to deal with both problems has been the creation of a residual category which falls outside of the social structure as it is conventionally understood; the 'underclass'. This concept does more than provide a social category which might contain, if not resolve, the analytical problem, for it has acquired a sense both pejorative and threatening. In much of its usage, those to whom the label is applied not only stand outside of mainstream society and its central institutions, they reject its underlying norms and values.

In Victorian England these social outsiders were sometimes termed the dangerous classes. They are now doubly dangerous, posing not only a threat to social organisation, but also a challenge to our models for portraying and understanding social structure. Through the construction of a category of 'outsiders', this threat is located outside of society, which may then be perceived as internally cohesive and free from significant challenge. Such a view of the social structure is by no means new, and in the nineteenth century suspicion and condemnation of the redundant population, the lumpenproletariat, the street folk, the social outcasts, the residuum, and the dangerous classes was common. Chapter 1 reviews these images, also examining the sorts of explanations offered in the accounts of the time. The emphasis was on moral failure, and sometimes poor socialisation, but often with the implicit suggestion of a different breed of person. By the end of the century a much more explicitly genetic approach had developed, championed by the eugenics movement, and taken up by the Fabians as a basis for social engineering.

There has always been a problem of classification in treatments of this social residuum; that of distinguishing between the worthy and unworthy poor. Much of the early British provision for the poor was built around this division. By the twentieth century, especially after the war effort and the consequent diminution of the 'social problem group', there was great optimism about the expected achievements of the welfare state. The ambitions of the social policy of the time are summed up in Marshall's (1950) notion of 'social citizenship': the guarantee of full social inclusion for all. The concept of social citizenship stands then as a counterpart to that of the underclass; the promise of social inclusion, as opposed to moral and material exclusion.

Chapter 2 traces the development of the British welfare state, and the centrality of the worthy/unworthy distinction. This distinction is inevitable in policy which seeks to make provision for the poor, but also to maintain the work ethic, a tension clearly present in contemporary systems of social security. At the time of the Beveridge plan it must have seemed that guaranteed social citizenship was a feasible objective, but its implementation quickly ran into a number of difficulties. Firstly, there was the distinction between means tested and contributory benefit; only the latter was granted unconditionally, while the former required an invasion of privacy and carried a greater social stigma. Secondly, there was the question of the rate of benefit which would ensure social inclusion, but without undermining the incentive to work. In practice, the guarantee of social citizenship carries with it the requirement of being willing and available for employment, and the policing of social security to this end has contributed to the stigma attaching to claimants. What was intended as a guarantee of inclusion has turned into a badge of exclusion.

The continuing presence of a marginalised or excluded group, currently termed the underclass, has been construed as a challenge to the achievement and objectives of the welfare state. On the one hand provision may be seen to have failed in its objective of guaranteed social inclusion for all, on the other hand the welfare state may be argued to have gone too far, to have proffered too many rights and extracted too few obligations. It is thus argued to have created a culture of dependency in a population which explicitly denies the norms and values of the society to which they notionally belong. These ideas have been most fully developed and argued in the US, and Chapter 3 examines the construction of the American welfare state, highlighting contrasts with Britain. Although the British approach initially served as a model in America, the system which eventually emerged in the mid-twentieth century showed some fundamental differences. The one which most concerns us here is the failure to provide long term provision for unemployed men as of right, and the reliance instead upon Aid to Families with Dependent Children (AFDC) as the major means tested provision.

AFDC principally acts as a means of support to single mothers, and is at the heart of an extensive literature which argues that welfare provision has gone too far, and is undermining the institution of the family. Dependence on welfare has become the major defining feature of the American 'underclass', made up of state dependent single mothers, and young males (predominantly black) who have withdrawn from the labour force and live on the criminal fringe. These young blacks are also assumed to have access to welfare, for which they themselves are not eligible, through their relationships with female claimants. The next generation is then argued to be brought up with a deviant set of attitudes and values, and the family task of socialisation to have been undermined. A new literature has emerged stressing not the rights but the obligations of citizenship, the principal obligation being to work in return for support. An alternative view asks what loyalties or duties are owed to a society which has so manifestly failed to deliver its promise, and what kind of citizenship it is which demands menial labour in low grade work paying insufficient for subsistence.

The notion of the underclass has been adopted, or resurrected, to capture the sense of a group which is excluded, or has withdrawn, from mainstream society, in terms of both style of life and the dominant system of morality. Chapter 4 examines the contemporary debate in both the British and American literature. Minimally the underclass is defined in terms of state dependence, and culturally based accounts of the phenomenon are expressed in terms of socialisation into an alternative system of values in which the single parent family is directly implicated. An alternative view stresses the structural processes underlying the emergence of an underclass, notably economic restructuring and the failure of the economies of both Britain and the US to generate sufficient jobs to accommodate all potential workers. The debate about the underclass has been led by a predominantly American literature, and as a result the position of the black population is a central concern. Within a broadly structural approach, however, there are disagreements about whether issues of class or race should be given primacy in explanation.

Wilson (1987) argues for a class based account, supporting this view by the assertion that the civil rights movement has removed the traditional barriers to black social mobility and that the position of the black underclass is to be explained by their vulnerability to job loss in manufacturing, rather than to racism. Fainstein (1992) challenges this view, arguing that the black population at all levels of the social structure still suffers impediments to mobility by virtue of racial discrimination, and that the position of the lowest stratum is by no means explained simply by their concentration in manufacturing in an increasingly service based economy. It is rather, he argues, that a generally weak position in the labour market is bred of disadvantage rooted in ethnic identity. The very high concentration of single parent households in the black population adds a further strand to the debate; this is seen either as the result of a culture of dependency which also explains black withdrawal from the labour force through a failure to instil the work ethic, or as the result of poor employment opportunities for black males.

These arguments do not easily transfer to the British situation, partly because of the difference in the welfare systems of the two countries. Although there has been a growth of single parenthood in Britain it is on nothing like the same scale as in the US, and the alleged emergence of a dependency culture has been applied rather to long term unemployment. Nor is the British underclass, however defined, predominantly a black phenomenon, largely because of the very much smaller size of the British black population. Nevertheless, a good deal of the British debate has revolved around predictions that Britain is following the same path as the US. There is also a considerable literature addressing specific aspects of the design and operation of the British benefit system, most notably with reference to the work incentive.

A dimension of the British debate that is absent from American literature and is firmly rooted in a major tradition of British sociology, is the challenge which long term unemployment and changing patterns of employment pose for conceptualisations of social structure. Conventional accounts of the British class structure have been based on schema derived from skill and occupational rankings, premised upon the norm of full employment. Long term unemployment minimally poses the problem of how to classify the unemployed, though it potentially challenges a view of social structure based solely upon occupational ranking. A further challenge is posed by the changing nature of employment and the phenomenon of what is often termed underemployment: chronic insecurity and non-standard patterns of work.

Thus the study of economic change uncovers patterns not easily incorporated into standard class analysis, and one response is to contain the troublesome features in the residual category of the underclass. Further problems arise, however, over the constitution of this category. Does it refer to all unemployed, the long term unemployed only, the underemployed or those dependent on the state for their livelihood? Arguments for each of these positions are reviewed in Chapter 4, where it becomes clear that in fact two different types of social distinction are operating. Dependence upon the state is a civic status, and one which often carries with it a social stigma, although it does not embrace a homogeneous collection of conditions. Social class position, in contrast, is rooted in the system of production. Unemployment, however, much less underemployment, cannot be accommodated simply by a designation beneath or outside of class; at least not without some consideration of the underlying dynamics of the labour market.

Issues concerning the structure of the labour market also arise in Chapter 5, which considers the nature and significance of gender differentiation in the underclass debate. Whilst this topic is ever present in substance, rarely is it made explicit in analysis. The most obvious example of the salience of gender is in work which attributes the reproduction of an underclass to the alleged failure of the single mother household in the task of socialisation, partially to be attributed to the absence of an appropriate male role model. Just as non-work is marginalised with reference to the social structure, single parenthood is marginalised with reference to the nuclear family ideal. Such an account might seem to suggest that the woman's role lies simply in the reproduction of an essentially male underclass. Their high level of state dependence, however, places most single mothers themselves firmly inside the defining criteria of the underclass. This then raises the question of societal expectations of women and mothers generally, but specifically of single mothers.

One account argues that society as a whole, and men in particular, are simply shifting the burden of poverty on to a specifically female population, and that the explanation of the high incidence of impoverished single parent households lies with the high levels of male unemployment. Other analyses are more critical of the women themselves, and argue for some work requirement to be imposed as a condition of benefit, which is in fact the situation in the US. This, however, brings women's socialisation role and work role into conflict, and also raises the question of their labour market vulnerability. In both Britain and America the principal reason that more single mothers are not in employment is because they are not in a position to earn sufficient to maintain a family and also cater for their child care needs. A similar dilemma is posed for the wives of unemployed men, who only rarely take over the 'breadwinning' role.

Thus the gender related issues which arise from the debate about the underclass stem from unresolved questions about the sexual division of labour in society. The assumption of a traditional arrangement between the sexes underlies the welfare systems of both Britain and the US, though there have been some changes in recent years. Nevertheless in both countries there is a complex interaction between state provision, gender ideology and the structure of the labour market which militates against a real challenge to established gender roles (Morris, 1990). Any require-ment that single mothers take paid employment brings family values and the work ethic into direct conflict, and touches on a problem for the idea of social citizenship. This is not an explicitly gendered notion, which is one of its failings. It is a concept of the public sphere, and stands as a counterpart to the notion of the underclass. But to address the issue of women's social inclusion and to resolve the tension between family values and the work ethic, the concept of social citizenship must also extend to the private sphere, the source of many of the constraints experienced by women in the public domain.

There is another sense in which the idea of social citizenship is too narrowly conceived, and that is in relation to the constitution of the social community. Migrant labour has generally been used as a means of creating a population of outsiders whose full membership of the receiving society is in some way questionable. The definition and control of outsiders in this context is to some degree bound up with the control of resources, and part of this process lies in establishing the terms and conditions of their entry, a matter of current debate with regard to the free movement of labour in Europe. These 'terms and conditions' are important with respect to two separate but related matters: the claim that migrants are to be allowed to make on the welfare state, and the position they occupy in the labour market. Chapter 6 provides some discussion of labour migration in these terms, and outlines some connections to be made with the concept of the underclass and of social citizenship.

The most vulnerable position is that of the illegal or clandestine migrant, who has no official existence in the receiving country, can make no claims for protection on either the legal system or the welfare system, and who is forced into employment which would be rejected by any with alternative means of support. In a slightly stronger position are the guest workers, or migrants allowed entry on condition of employment. These workers are essentially expendable, and recruited on this understanding, although in practice they have not been so easily disposed of. Whilst colonial migrants have often had access to European labour markets as full citizens, ethnic and racial discrimination have usually limited their prospects. Each of these categories tends to be confined to low-paid, menial and insecure employment, but in this they differ from the 'underclass' as commonly defined: a category of state dependants.

The relationship between the 'underclass' and menial migrant labour is an interesting one. The migrant group cannot, without some adjustment of thinking, be included in an underclass defined in terms of non-employment, but are often confined to jobs which would not be contemplated by full citizens of the receiving country. This fact can be, and has been, held to demonstrate the lack of work incentive among the underclass; support for the view that welfare provision is too generous and is keeping people out of work. The counter-argument is that the guarantee of social citizenship should include the right to certain minimum conditions in employment, and the right to reject work which falls below that level. Migrant labour provides a source of workers who, lacking other means of support, have no such rights, and some writers have suggested that in this respect they themselves constitute an underclass.

Migrant labour is an issue which falls outside the usual terms of reference of the contemporary debate about the underclass, but serves to highlight a number of important points. One is the interaction between the structure and operation of the labour market and the guarantees offered by social citizenship. Recent debate has asked in what circumstances social citizenship should guarantee at least basic maintenance, and what minimum conditions of employment should an individual be able to demand? The emerging emphasis on duties alongside rights asserts that there are limits to the protections to be guaranteed by social citizenship. The target groups for the imposition of tighter social obligations are state dependent single mothers, America's disadvantaged black population, and Britain's long term unemployed. The position of migrant labourers with minimal rights, however, illustrates what the implications of such a shift might be.

The general consensus on the definition of the underclass is that it should include only the non-employed and state dependent, but how far can any understanding of this group be reached in isolation from an examination of the operation of the labour market, and the practical and political constraints which influence the design and administration of welfare policy? Broadening the framework to encompass these issues would allow us to integrate in one discussion the position of women, the experience of migrant workers, the circumstances of the black population, the dilemma of the long term unemployed, etc. But how far does the notion of the underclass help in this endeavour? Does the current debate simply reproduce the limitations and errors of thinking of one hundred years ago, or do the same ideas reappear across time because they contain some fundamental truth?

Chapter 1

Dangerous classes

There has been a recent growth of speculation and debate about the emergence of an underclass in British and American society. This concept remains ill-defined, as the following chapters will demonstrate, but broadly speaking it rests upon the assertion that there exist certain groupings which fall, in some sense, outside of an otherwise cohesive and integrated society. The idea will sometimes involve a biological argument, sometimes a moral judgement, sometimes a view of changing class structure, and sometimes the idea of inadequate socialisation and a deviant 'sub-culture'. Whilst currently experiencing some kind of revival, the notion of a substratum, residuum, or 'underclass' has been remarkably tenacious throughout the history of industrial society, and in this chapter we review some of its forerunners in British social thought.

THE REDUNDANT POPULATION

T.R. Malthus, writing in England at the turn of the eighteenth century, expressed concern about the 'redundant population', resulting from an excess of births over deaths, which he attributed to three immediate causes: the prolificness of marriages; the proportion of those born who lived to marry; and the earliness of these marriages compared with life expectation (Malthus, 1806; reprinted 1989: 11). Whilst he argued that the problem of over-population would always eventually be resolved by some natural disaster, an 'inevitable law of nature', his concern was to find a solution with 'the least possible prejudice to the virtue and happiness of human society' (1989: 87). The answer, he believed, lay in 'self-restraint', for 'If we multiply too fast we die miserably of poverty and contagious diseases' (1989: 88).

The poor, who suffer most from the effects of overpopulation, are, he argued, deluded as to the cause of their poverty:

> When the wages of labour are hardly sufficient to maintain two children, a man marries and has five or six. He of course finds himself miserably distressed. He accuses the insufficiency of the price of labour to maintain a family. He accuses his parish for their tardy and sparing fulfilment of their obligation to assist him. He accuses the avarice of the rich, who suffer him to want what they can so well spare. He accuses the partial and unjust institutions of society, which have awarded him an inadequate share of the produce of the earth. He accuses perhaps the dispensations of Providence, which have assigned him a place in society so beset with unavoidable distress and dependence. In searching for objects of accusation, he never adverts to the quarter from which all his misfortunes originate. The last person he would think of accusing is himself. (1989: 106)

For Malthus the problems of the poor follow directly from their giving in to natural passions which require regulation and direction, and it is the containment of these desires which holds the key to the elimination of poverty and disease. His ideal situation would be that in which man retained a strong desire to marry, but delayed until he had good prospects of supporting a wife and children. His recommendations are therefore to restrict support for the poor, and to do nothing which might encourage marriage, or destroy the 'inequality of circumstances' between a single man and a man with a family. The proper check to population size is moral restraint, for the children of the poor go on to reproduce their own misery: 'educated in workhouses where every vice is propagated, or bred up at home in filth and rags, and with an utter ignorance of every moral obligation' (p. 112). Hence, morality is seen as the basis of a good society, and moral failure the cause of poverty and distress.

For Malthus it was important that the poor be made to recognise and accept responsibility for their circumstances, and be educated out of their habit of attributing distress to the failure of the rulers of society. 'The circulation of Paine's Rights of Man . . . has done great mischief among the lower and middling classes of people in this country' (p. 126). A call for greater public provision for the poor may be expressed in terms of liberty and justice, he argues, but in practice raises unrealistic expectations. The result is to release demand for impossible change, which can only be contained by military despotism. An ignorance of the true source of poverty is seen as unfavourable to the cause of civil liberty, with the expectation of government support inevitably provoking irritation against those more securely placed.

The case for raising wages in relation to the cost of living as a means of curbing poverty is also rejected, for the workers themselves are argued to hold the potential for controlling wages; by restricting their own numbers they could force up the price of labour. Malthus does, however, maintain that some imbalance between population size and the availability of resources is necessary to overcome the 'acknowledged indolence of man' (1989: 93), for without the spur of scarcity the will to work would disappear. This fragile will to work he also felt to be threatened by assistance for the poor, so that the Poor Laws perpetuate rather than resolve the problem of poverty. Even the idea of a contributory insurance system was not well received by Malthus, who argues, as it turns out with some validity, that such schemes give the illusion of security which they cannot provide because demand will eventually outstrip resources. The worthy impulse of benevolence is seen to be ultimately destructive: 'We shall raise the worthless above the worthy; we shall encourage indolence and check industry; and, in the most marked manner subtract from the sum of human happiness' (p. 157).

Contained in the work of Malthus on the 'redundant population' we find a set of inter-related ideas which will become quite familiar in the course of this book. Poverty is brought upon the sufferer by *his* own failure; the idea of state responsibility is politically disruptive, dishonest, and likely to end in despotism; poverty is spread by a sub-culture based on vice, filth and moral ignorance; public provision for the poor destroys the will to work; man is naturally indolent; the resolution to the problem lies in moral education and the enforcement of self-reliance.

Such ideas were common at the beginning of the nineteenth century, and Carlyle, though overtly opposed to Malthusianism, gives perhaps the strongest expression of the importance of self-reliance. 'For the idle man there is no place in this England of ours. . . . He that will not work according to his faculty, let him perish according to his necessity: there is no juster law than that' (n.d.: 177). The New Poor Law of 1834 embodied similar sentiments in the principle of less eligibility: 'The situation of the individual relieved must not be made really or apparently so eligible as the situation of the independent labourer of the lowest class.' It was argued in the Poor Law Report that the state of dependency itself produced a population 'callous to its own degradation', thus the failure to work was a moral failure and dependency the cause of moral degeneration.

THE RELATIVE SURPLUS AND THE LUMPENPROLETARIAT

By the latter half of the nineteenth century Marx was to issue a direct rebuttal of the Malthusian explanation of poverty, but in doing so to offer an account which nevertheless carried its own moral message. In the second volume of his *Critique of Political Economy* Marx wrote of:

The folly of the economic pundits who urge the workers to adapt their numbers to capital's need for self-expansion. . . . The mechanism of capitalist production and accumulation continually adapts the number of the workers to capital's need for self-expansion. The first word of this adaptation is the creation of relative surplus population, or an industrial reserve army; the last word is the poverty of continually increasing strata of the active labour army, and the dead weight of pauperism. (1930: 713)

He was not, however, in complete disagreement with Malthus, for: 'Although Malthus, in his narrow minded fashion, regards overpopulation as due to an absolute excess of growth of the working population, and not as due to a merely relative superfluity, he nonetheless recognises that overpopulation is necessary to modern industry' (p. 700).

This excess population is described sometimes in Malthusian terms as 'redundant', or as surplus, but is argued by Marx to perform a vital function in capitalist society. Elasticity of capital, the availability of credit, the increase in social wealth, and the technologically enhanced productivity of labour all contribute to a fund of capital 'urgently seeking investment', and thus dependent on 'great masses' of available labour. By forming an industrial reserve army, this population 'becomes a lever promoting capital accumulation'. These masses serve not only to support expansions in production, but also through the threat of competition, to exert a pressure on the working population which spurs them on to overwork, and 'subjects them more completely to the dictatorship of capital'. The expansion and contraction of the industrial reserve army helps to regulate the general movement of wages, which are determined not by absolute numbers of workers, but by the relative sizes of the active and reserve army of labour.

According to Marx the relative surplus population of the unemployed or partially employed exists in three forms: floating, latent and stagnant. The floating surplus is made up of young workers who are dismissed when they reach *manhood*. Even workers who remain in relatively secure employment through their adult years become superfluous as they age, for the middle-aged worker is apt to be 'worn out' by the demands of industrial employment. The latent surplus derives from the rural population, released 'as capitalist production [masters] the domain of agriculture'. The stagnant surplus is that part of active labour whose employment is 'extremely irregular . . . characterised by working hours of extreme length for wages of extreme lowness' (p. 710). In writing of this latter grouping Marx highlights an issue which in subsequent years became a major source of social concern, and which prompted much of the debate surrounding the 'surplus population'. 'This stagnant section of the reserve army . . . forms a self-perpetuating and self-reproducing element of the working class, and it takes a proportionally greater part in the general increase of that class than do other elements' (p. 711).

The lowest sediment of the reserve population – which specifically excludes vagrants, criminals and prostitutes – 'dwells in the world of pauperism . . . the tatterdemalion and slum proletariat' (p. 711), and is made up of a further three categories: the able-bodied without work, orphans and pauper children, and the demoralised, degenerate and unemployable. 'Pauperism constitutes the infirmary of the active labour army . . . but capital knows how to shift this burden, for the most part, from its own shoulders to those of the working class and the lower middle class' (p. 712).

Though self-reproducing, a burden to society, and living lives of misery, this surplus population is, for Marx, an inescapable feature of capitalist society, for:

> The accumulation of wealth at one pole of society involves a simultaneous accumulation of poverty, labour torment, slavery, ignorance, brutalisation, and moral degradation, at the opposite

pole – where dwells the class that produces its own product in the form of capital. (p. 714)

In opposition to Malthus, Marx offers an account of unemployment, underemployment and poverty in terms of the dynamic of capitalism, rather than individual morality. The reserve population may thus be termed the necessary casualties of capitalism. Moral condemnation appears, however, in his treatment of the lumpenproletariat, whom he sharply distinguishes from the reserve army or surplus:[1]

'This scum of the depraved elements of all classes' (a);

'The dangerous class, the social scum, that passively rotting mass thrown off by the lowest layers of the old society' (b);

'The lumpenproletariat, which in all big towns forms a mass sharply differentiated from the industrial proletariat, a recruiting ground for thieves and criminals of all kinds living on the crumbs of society, people without a definite trade, vagabonds, *gens sans feu et sans aveu*' (c);

'decayed roués . . . vagabonds, discharged soldiers, discharged jailbirds, escaped galley slaves, swindlers, mountebanks, lazzaroni, pickpockets, tricksters, gamblers, maquereaus, brothel keepers, porters, literati, organ-grinders, ragpickers, knife grinders, tinkers, beggars – in short the whole indefinite, disintegrated mass, thrown hither and thither, which the French term *la bohème*' (d).

Bovenkerk (1984) has documented the inconsistent use by Marx of the term lumpenproletariat, which may variously refer to an historical remnant from an earlier society, a group of individual social degenerates, or a category located outside of the economic system of industrial capitalism, whilst Bussard (1987) notes a similarity with traditional European attitudes towards the poor. In fact, Marx's writing reflects the morality of his times. Here in the lumpenproletariat we are presented with an entirely blameworthy, immoral and degenerate mass, a category which differs from the surplus cast off by the industrial machinery of capitalism, standing apart from the 'real workers' of the proletariat (Bussard, 1987). Marx's disdain seems to be rooted in part in the lack of any potential for collective class awareness in this grouping, but also betrays a condemnation of their individual morality.

This moral and economic marginality is a recurrent theme in

much of the writing on the underclass, but beneath this issue lies the question of whether the concept has any validity as a tool of social analysis. The questions which are central to contemporary debate about the underclass are already present in these samples of thought more than a hundred years old: does the explanation of poverty and idleness lie in the economic structure or in personal morality; does state responsibility for poverty encourage dependency and degradation; is there a homogeneous social grouping which lies outside society's norms, values and economic structures? The identification of such a grouping, and the need for its integration or elimination, came to dominate social thought in the latter half of nineteenth century England, just as it has reappeared at the end of the twentieth century.

THE LONDON STREET FOLK

By the middle of the nineteenth century the separation of the respectable working class from a substratum of social outcasts had become a major concern for London society, and a moral ambiguity is present in many accounts of the period. Mayhew's work is distinctive in being fully grounded in an understanding of the nature of the London labour market, which offered little secure industrial employment. Casual work and seasonal employment were endemic, and there was a glut of unskilled labour, swollen by the influx of population from the countryside (Stedman-Jones, 1984). Much of Mayhew's early writing, for a series of articles in the *Morning Chronicle* beginning in 1848, and finally appearing as *London Labour and the London Poor* (1861), provided detail of casual and sweated work, and a sympathetic view of its victims' apparently undisciplined behaviour. Mayhew understood that 'All casual labour . . . is necessarily uncertain labour, and wherever uncertainty exists, there can be no foresight or providence' (1861, II: 325), and saw that 'Regularity of habits are incompatible with irregularity of income . . . it is a moral impossibility that a class of labourers who are only occasionally employed should be either generally industrious or temperate' (1861, III: 309).

Below even the casually employed and sweated labourers he identifies the self-employed London street folk, and finally the 'social outcasts', though the distinction between these two categories is somewhat blurred. The former include 'street sellers, street finders, street performers, street artisans, street labourers', and the latter 'prostitutes, thieves, swindlers and beggars'. Stedman-Jones (1984: 89) has commented on the problem of distinguishing vagrants from ordinary casual labourers, for the former can be drawn into temporary labour with seasonal demand, and their situation may anyway be the result of the vagaries of the labour market. Mayhew, however, leans towards a moral and biological account, dividing humanity broadly into two races: the wanderers and the settlers; the vagabond and the citizen; the nomadic and the civilised tribes. The whole of the rootless category is seen as a race apart, a wandering tribe, sharing a love of the roving life, a repugnance towards civilisation, and a psychological incapacity for steady work.

In contrast with his sympathy for the casual worker Mayhew asserts: 'The nomad . . . is distinguished from the civilized man by his repugnance to regular and continuous labour – by his want of providence in laying up store for the future – by his inability to perceive consequences ever so slightly removed from immediate apprehension' (1861, I: 2). Thus Mayhew's structural understanding of the London labour market sits uneasily with a focus on individual predispositions, captured in his opposition between the vagrant and the citizen. The former group shares: 'a greater development of the animal than of the intellectual or moral nature', 'high cheekbones and protruding jaws', 'slang language', 'lax ideas about property', 'general improvidence', 'repugnance to continuous labour', 'disregard of female honour', 'love of cruelty', 'pugnacity', 'an utter want of religion', 'extreme animal fondness for the opposite sex' (cited in Himmelfarb, 1984: 325).

They are described as socially, morally, and perhaps even physically distinct; a race apart. Though Mayhew makes particular reference to the Irish and the Jews, the wandering category as a whole is set in opposition to the civilised population: 'Paupers, beggars and outcasts, possessing nothing but what they acquire by depredation from the industrious, provident, and civilized portion of the community'. He felt he had identified a distinctive physical, mental and moral constitution, and argued, 'It is curious that no one has yet applied the above facts to the explanation of certain anomalies in the present state of society among ourselves' (1861, I: 2–3).

There was more pity for some than for others, however, 'according as they will work, they can't work, and they won't work'. Those who were born to the street and those who were

driven there, were deemed more deserving than those who chose
the street. For many, Mayhew argued, street life was adopted
'From a horror of the workhouse, and a disposition to do at least
something for the food they eat' (1861, IV: 322–3). Those born to
the street, however, were felt to share a particular cultural
predisposition, 'imbibing the habits and the morals of the gutters
almost with their mother's milk . . . the child without training goes
back to its parent stock the vagabond savage' (1861, I: 320), a view
reminiscent of Malthus' passage: 'bred up in vice and ignorance'.

Mayhew's intention was to plead the cause of these people, who
are termed 'an evil of our own making', 'a national disgrace to us
all', and who were to be looked upon more with pity than with
anger. Yet they were described in terms that condemn, as 'a foul
disgrace', 'living in an utterly creedless, mindless and principleless
state', 'the lowest depths of barbarism', 'beasts of the field',
'instinctless animals'. He certainly identifies them as a class apart:
'I am anxious that the public should no longer confound the
honest, independent working men, with the vagrant beggars and
pilferers of this country; and that they should see that the one class
is as respectable and worthy as the other is degraded and vicious'
(1861, III: 371). Yet by his own account of the market for labour
a line between the casual labourer and the vagrant cannot be so
easily drawn.

His description is not primarily of an economic category but a
moral and biological one; the relation of the street folk and the
social outcasts to employment was thus seen to be incidental to
these features, rather than the cause of them. Their circumstances
were reported in such a way that the individuals became associated
with the conditions:

> As the streets grow blue with the coming light . . . they come
> sauntering forth, the unwashed poor, some with greasy wallets
> on their back, to haunt over each dirt heap, and eke out life by
> seeking refuse, bones or stray rags and pieces of old iron.
> (*Morning Chronicle*, Oct. 1849, quoted in Himmelfarb, 1984:
> 318)

There are similiarities in other documents of the time. For
example the *Report on the Sanitary Conditions of the Labouring
Poor* (1842) refers to 'the residuum' as refuse and offal, whilst one
eyewitness report of bone pickers describes them as follows:
'Often hardly human in appearance, they had neither human

tastes nor sympathies, not even human sensations, for they revelled in the filth which is grateful to dogs.' A structural location is thus combined with a moral condemnation and racial distancing fuelled by the curiosity and social fears of the established middle-class population.

THE RESIDUUM

Stedman-Jones (1984) depicts the period from 1860 to 1880 as one of the demoralisation and remoralisation of the poor. In other words, the explanation of poverty is deemed to lie in moral failure, and its solution in moral education. Public relief and indiscriminate charity were held to blame, and the insecurity which characterised the London labour market was rarely considered:

> No such concession was made to the problems of the casual labourer; if he begged that was because he was demoralised; if he was unemployed that was because he was not really interested in work; if he congregated together with others of his kind in poor areas that was because he was attracted by the prospect of charitable hand-outs. (Stedman-Jones, 1984: 262)

Poverty was seen as the outward manifestation of demoralisation: 'The expectation of alms from private charity or from the rates attracts a redundant population to the metropolis, and then induces them to hang on at half work' (Denison, 1872, quoted in Stedman-Jones, 1984: 267). Their poverty is thus bred of their moral failure.

Stedman-Jones argues that the greater prosperity of the 1870s as compared with the 1860s awakened an optimism about the prospects of remoralising the poor, to be based in part on the restriction of aid. Notable examples of this endeavour are found in the work of Octavia Hill and of the Charity Organisation Society: 'The general aim of these activities was to impose upon the life of the poor a system of sanctions and rewards which would convince them that there would be no escape from life's miseries except by thrift, regularity and hard work' (Stedman-Jones, 1984: 271).

The work of the social explorers (e.g. Mearns, 1883; Sims, 1883) testified to the continuing misery of the poor, however, and the return of harsh economic conditions in the 1880s seems to have marked a further shift in attitudes, particularly focused upon both the size and concentration of the 'residuum'.

One specific aspect of concern was the housing crisis of the 1880s, and the overcrowding and corruption it was argued to entail:

> Often in the family of an honest working man, compelled to take refuge in a thieves kitchen . . . there can be no question that numbers of habitual criminals would never have become such, had they not by force of circumstances been packed together in these slums with those who were hardened in crime. (Mearns, 1883: 1)

The residuum was thus held to corrupt or contaminate those in the class immediately above, and a policy of dispersal was consequently advocated in the form of labour encampments outside London. Stedman-Jones (1984: 305) cites the following piece from the *Spectator* on the Toynbee Commission's solutions to the situation in the East End (1892):

> Those that sign the report see that their scheme will be no permanent remedy, unless they can separate the 'unemployed' from those out of employ, or, as they put it, the 'demoralised residuum' from those 'with whom it is possible to deal hopefully'; and they actually declare that the former cannot be treated as bonafide unemployed.

The solution was the denial of any support other than compulsory work in industrial regiments. Assisted emigration was also suggested, though Samuel Smith's response graphically conveys the sentiment of the times: 'While the flower of the population emigrate, the residuum stays, corrupting and being corrupted, like the sewage of the metropolis which remained floating at the mouth of the Thames last summer' (quoted in Stedman-Jones, 1984: 309).

Despite the potential of the residuum to corrupt, it was also claimed that part of the problem was the absence of the improving influence of the superior classes. Already by the mid-nineteenth century the idea of a society deeply divided into two opposing groups had become a commonplace. As early as 1831 Carlyle wrote: 'Wealth has accumulated itself into masses, and Poverty, also in accumulation enough, lies impassably separated from it; opposed, uncommunicating, like forces in positive and negative poles' (quoted in Keating, 1976: 11).

This notion of a dramatic social fissure between the poor and 'the rest' was also caught in Disraeli's metaphor of 'two nations between whom there is no intercourse and no sympathy' (1845). With the extension of the franchise in 1867 and 1884 there was a growing fear of the political power which could be wielded by those living in the abyss of poverty.

Marx and Engels (1848) had already written of the importance of spatial concentrations of the working class for the realisation of a collective identity and the enhancement of political action. 'Society as a whole is more and more splitting up into two great hostile camps, two great classes directly facing each other: Bourgeoisie and Proletariat.' The urban middle classes were equally aware of these possibilities and the threat of 'mob rule'. The political nature of this fear is caught in these remarks by Gladstone in 1877:

> The town populations dwell in masses closely wedged together, and they habitually assemble in crowds for the purposes of many of their occupations. It is in this state of juxtaposition that political electricity flies from man to man with a violence which displaces judgement from its seat and carries off individual minds in a flood by the resistless rush of sympathy. (Stedman-Jones, 1984: 151)

Pick (1989) quotes from the *Spectator* (1891) on 'the collective inhumanity of a great number of people', and 'the shameless cowardice of the crowd'; 'a whole body of men, collected at hazard, who on occasions will prove themselves more mercilessly cruel than a pack of wolves that tears to pieces and devours the fallen or wounded of its number'.

Moral condemnation of the poor was to prove remarkably tenacious, despite the growth of an increasingly sympathetic documentation of their circumstances. Booth's work made a new departure in attempting a definition of poverty and in developing reliable methods of measurement and classification. Although his approach has since been subject to much criticism, his work marked a watershed in social research and in the state of knowledge on the extent and nature of poverty in Victorian England.

Booth's survey of London in the 1880s found one-third (30.7 per cent) of the population to be living in poverty, and included along with the indigent a substantial number of the labouring poor. Potentially, says Himmelfarb (1984), this finding 're-moralized' the poor, and challenged any clearcut division between the respectable poor and the residuum. The corrupting influence and moral failure of Booth's lowest class, however, remain: 'Occasional labourers, street-sellers, loafers, criminals and semi-criminals. . . . They degrade whatever they touch and as individuals are incapable of improvement' (Keating, 1976: 114).

It is worth noting here that a later distinction by Rowntree (1901) between primary and secondary poverty also encouraged moral judgement, in that secondary poverty was attributed to 'drink, betting and gambling' and 'ignorant and careless house-keeping', such that 'Rowntree was partly responsible for the ease with which, for instance, the *Times* was able to conclude that the larger proportion of poor "were miserable mainly from their own fault"' (Vincent, 1991: 2).

SOCIAL DARWINISM

Despite an uncertain division between the casual labourer and the vagrant, the sense of the poor as a race apart was clear from Mayhew's writing, and was present in the popular novels of the time. Himmelfarb (1984) cites Ainsworth's Jack Sheppard in a novel of the same name (1839), whose physical appearance marked him out as a villain, found among 'the dregs of society', the 'lowest order of insolvent traders, thieves, mendicants, and other worthless and nefarious characters', 'the superfluous villainy of the metropolis'. Thus, argues Himmelfarb, 'There is never any doubt of Jack's irreclaimable nature. By character, heritage, environment and will, he is a member of the "dangerous classes"' (p. 427).

Towards the end of the century a position developed which focused as much on physical degeneration as on demoralisation. Longstaffe (1893) writes in the *Journal of the Royal Statistical Society*, 'The narrow chest, the pale eyes, the weak eyes, the bad teeth, of the town-bred children are but too apparent . . . long life in the town is accompanied by more or less degeneration of the race.' These views were often expressed in Darwinian terms, and the idea became current that the urban environment actually selected and favoured a particularly inferior breed of humanity, 'a race of men, small, ill-formed, disease-stricken, hard to kill' (Searle, 1976: 25). Images such as these struck fear into the heart of the secure and respectable population in the latter half of the nineteenth century, and fuelled the fire of the eugenics movement. Here we see fears of social disorder, of a burden on the public purse, and of immorality, tied together with ideas about hereditary degeneration, and the popularised influence of 'social Darwinism'.

Like Malthus, Darwin was concerned with overpopulation. This, together with other pressures on the survival of the individuals in a given species, was argued to spark off a process of natural selection. The features of any particular individual which give them a better chance of survival would be perpetuated in the next generation and thus become characteristic of the species as a whole. At about the same time, Jones (1980) argues, there was an impulse pushing social scientists towards a science of human character, which would include both physiology and social behaviour, making at least a tentative link between the two. This impulse is not solely attributable to Darwin, she suggests, but was already present in the works of Comte and Spencer. Darwin's theory of natural selection, however, slotted into a set of ideas already embracing the notion of progression in social change.

This developmental assumption was not apparent in the early work of Darwin, who argued that the 'unfit' in any one particular set of circumstances may well become the survivors in another. But this did not inhibit the appropriation and adaptation of Darwin's argument in speculation about human evolution: 'That righteous and salutary law of natural selection in virtue of which the best specimens of the race . . . continue the species and propagate an ever improving and perfecting type of humanity' (Greg, a liberal manufacturer in Victorian England, cited in Jones, 1980: 7). This was the spirit in which social Darwinism developed.

In a later work, *The Descent of Man* (1871), Darwin struggled to establish a theory of continuity between man and animals, arguing that basic human faculties existed in undeveloped form in animals. Elaborations of this link included a parallel psychological argument. Thus the development of the human race from the savage state up to that of modern man was compared with the mental development of a human child. Mental collapse then came to be seen as a form of psychological atavism: the surfacing of the characteristics of primitive ancestors. Though Darwin denied any necessary progression, there was a developmentalism implicit in his writing. 'Differences . . . between the highest man and the lowest savage are connected by the finest graduations. It is possible that they might pass and be developed into each other' (Jones, 1980: 17). The development of any animal with social instincts necessarily entailed the acquisition of a 'moral sense or conscience', as soon as intellectual powers permitted. Though morality was given a functional role by Darwin the argument inevitably seemed to support a view of progressive development that placed modern man at the top of a hierarchy. Purely physical evolution gave way to moral and mental evolution; demoralisation and degeneration could be seen to go hand in hand.

It is interesting that the 'doctrine of descent' was embraced both in the cause of socialism and also in the defence of hierarchy (see Pick, 1989: 28). It could be used to argue for the 'naturalness' of inequality in society, and the importance of allowing the sorting process to operate without impediment or interference. Alternatively it could be embraced by Marxists and socialists as offering an evolutionary rationale for their politics. There was, however, implicit in Darwin's writing a counterpart to the evolutionary progression of mankind, and that is the possibility of a deterioration or degeneration. 'Degenerescence' seems to have been firstly and most fully developed in Morel's (1857) writing in France (see Pick, 1989), largely in the predictions of deterioration through the uncontrolled expansion of the 'dangerous classes' made up of mentally, physically and morally inferior beings.

Such ideas also appeared in England, exemplified by the writings of Edwin Ray Lankester, author of *Degeneration. A Chapter in Darwinism* (1880). He was specifically concerned, as were many others, with the increasing urban population, a concern he later attributed in Malthusian terms to 'the early marriage and excessive reproduction of the reckless and hopeless, the poorest, least capable, least desirable members of the community' (1910, cited in Pick, 1989: 32). Debates such as these, most loosely linked to the original ideas propounded by Darwin, formed the context in which theories of heredity and an associated eugenics movement took root. The founder of this movement was Francis Galton (1822–1911), whose intention was that social administration and social policy should be informed and shaped by social Darwinism. His underlying proposition was that those in society with the more desirable physical and mental qualities should be identified and encouraged to multiply faster than the others – the 'reckless' and the 'hopeless'.

EUGENICS

Galton is another writer who in some sense addresses the ideas of Malthus, but he argued against voluntary restraint of reproduction, for this would lead to a decline in precisely those classes who benefit the population most: the prudent and more able classes (Kevles, 1985: 9). Galton's own position was that man was in the process of rising from an earlier barbarous state and should be helped on his way by policies for breeding out vestigial barbarism. His argument, of course, rested on the assertion that mental as well as physical attributes were hereditary, and this assertion was supported by the research of the German biologist, Weismann, in the late 1880s. The conclusions of his work suggested that the environment could have only limited effects in enhancing human qualities already present. It could not correct or compensate for their absence.

There followed, by the turn of the eighteenth century, a view that in England the lower classes were breeding more quickly than their social and moral superiors, and this would have a deleterious effect on society as a whole. Thus, argues Jones, 'Eugenics was able to integrate two aspects of late nineteenth century culture – fear of working class disorder and discontent and the rise in their numbers' (1980: 103). The implication of this view was to discount any collective social responsibility for social problems, for these were deemed to result from heredity. To support and comfort the poor was to encourage the reproduction of precisely that section of society which posed a threat to progressive evolutionary development.

Eugenics thus came 'More and more to represent the common sense of the middle classes. . . . As time progressed it became clearer that eugenics meant the preservation and increase of the middle classes' (Jones, 1980: 113). A series of prestigious public addresses marks Galton's rising influence; he gave the Huxley lecture in 1901, before the Anthropological Institute, and spoke both in 1904 and 1905 before the Sociological Society. After the panic over physical deterioration revealed in the course of recruiting for the Boer War, Galton's arguments found a ready audience. 'The casual residuum once more became the topic of anxious debate, provoked this time not by fears of revolution but intimations of impending imperial decline' (Stedman-Jones, 1984: 330).

The eugenicists' interest in social engineering brought them close to Fabian ideas about the creation of a better society, and social Darwinism was appropriated in a form not inconsistent with socialist values. Thus 'rational selection' rather than 'natural selection' was taken up as the basis for a new kind of society (D.G.

Ritchie, 1989). A concern with imperialism and national efficiency, as well as a more just social order underlay the Fabian interest in these ideas, though there was some confusion in their account of socially created but individually transmitted problems. Thus Sidney Webb (1896) is critical of competitive capitalism for its 'wrong production, both of commodities and of human beings', but nonetheless identified 'degenerate hordes of a demoralized "residuum" unfit for social life'. Elsewhere (1901) he saw the vitality of the race as being undermined by the physical and moral deterioration caused by sweated work, but despite this apparent appreciation of social explanations he saw the key to the problem as lying in the control of differential fertility rates. The population, it seemed, could be broadly divided between the desirable and undesirable; the former should be encouraged to reproduce and the latter group prevented. Thus, states Shaw, 'Social Darwinism, eugenics and Fabianism could have been made for each other' (1987: 543).

Official concern at around this time is reflected in the work of the Inter-Departmental Committee on Physical Deterioration in 1904. The recruiting officer's report at the time of the war had attributed the poor physical condition of the working class population to bad environment and inadequate diet. Whilst the Committee's findings showed little support for a strictly eugenicist view, one recommendation was for dispersal of the residuum and the formation of labour colonies. The final conclusion, however, defined the problem as 'ignorance and neglect on the part of the parents', with the ultimate solution argued to lie in 'some great scheme of social education to which many agencies must contribute: legislative, administrative and philanthropic, and by which the people themselves must be induced to cast off the paralysing traditions of helplessness and despair' (quoted in Vincent, 1991: 35); in other words, 'remoralisation'.

Others, however, notably Karl Pearson, had been active in propounding the argument that heredity was the self-evident basis of class position:

> If we look upon society as an organic whole, we must assume that class distinctions are not entirely illusory; that certain families pursue definite occupations, because they have a more or less specialised aptitude for them. In a rough sort of way we may safely assume that the industrial classes are not on the

average as intelligent as the professional classes and that the distinction is not entirely one of education. (Jones, 1980: 114)

Pearson's fear was that the 'worst' stocks in the population were increasing while the 'best' stocks were dying out. He predicted that 25 per cent of the population were producing 50 per cent of the next generation; and they were the wrong 25 per cent (Searle, 1976: 26).

Sidney Webb took up Pearson's position, adding a racial dimension:

> In Great Britain at this moment, when half or perhaps two thirds of all the married people are regulating their families, children are being freely born to the Irish Roman Catholics and the Polish, Russian and German Jews, on the one hand, and the thriftless and irresponsible – largely the casual labourers and other denizens of the one-roomed tenements of our great cities – on the other. . . . This can hardly result in anything but a national deterioration; or, as an alternative, this country falling to the Irish and the Jews. (1907, cited in Kevles, 1985: 74)

In fact racism figures to a lesser degree in British eugenics than in the United States, and Kevles (1985: 76) reports that the British movement contained a number of prominent Jewish members. Sensationalist prognostications rested on class differences and physical frailty more commonly than ethnic difference. 'If we go forward to the next generation there may be two thousand of them, and in the third generation twenty thousand of them! An army of epilectics, paralytics and tuberculates!' (Mudge, 1909: 95) These arguments supported an anti-welfare sentiment which held that provision for the poor caused 'Some partial arrest of that selective influence of struggle and competition' (Alfred Marshall, quoted in Jones, 1980: 114) The unfit were poised to overwhelm the fit.

Other commentators were beginning to place more stress on environmental than genetic factors. Pigou, for example, argued that the environment itself had lasting effects through future generations. The nature/nurture opposition was also taken up by the Commission on the Care and Control of the Feebleminded (1908):

> Two opposing doctrines have been submitted to us. (1) According to the one, mental defect is spontaneous in its beginnings

and has a great tendency to recur in descendants and thus is truly inborn. . . . (2) According to the other, the evil influences of the environment are far more important than the innate and spontaneous defect of mental capacity transmissible by inheritance.

As Jones puts it (1980: 116), 'Eugenics had in fact failed to totally convince', but this did not mean that the hopes and aims of the eugenicists were laid to rest.

THE SOCIAL PROBLEM GROUP

The onset of the First World War arguably demonstrated that the casual poor at least were a social not a biological creation (Stedman-Jones, 1971: 336). The biological school, however, did survive the war and in the 1920s there was a renewed interest in the 'social problem group'. One of the reasons behind this was the threat that mass democracy posed to existing class privileges. Blacker (1926) argues that the method of obtaining votes would necessarily lead to a response to the desire for welfare, regardless of the eugenic costs. There was strong opposition to social provisions, which protected the unfit who would otherwise fall prey to the forces of natural selection (C.V. Drysdale, in Ray 1983: 214), whilst the vying of political parties was thought to lead to competitive bribery of 'the great crowd of the unsuccessful'. Armstrong goes on to argue: 'Under democracy what hope is there of changing, even though the wiser among us begin to see whither it is leading? The inefficient will always outvote the efficient' (1931: 17–18). The appeal of eugenics, argues Ray (1983), was that it suggested a means of removing the social problem group whilst leaving the existing distribution of wealth unchanged.

The hard core of the group of social inefficients was considered to be constituted by the mental defectives (Macnicol, 1987), but the focus of concern was more broadly dispersed. The Wood Report on Mental Deficiency (*Report*, 1929: 81) states: 'If we are to deal with the racial disaster of mental deficiency, we must deal not merely with mentally defective persons, but with the whole subnormal group from which the majority of them come.' It was also argued that if empirically investigated, this group would be found to include:

a much larger proportion of insane persons, epileptics, paupers, criminals (especially recidivists), unemployables, habitual slum dwellers, prostitutes, inebriates and other social inefficients than would a group of families not containing mental defectives. The overwhelming majority of the families thus collected will belong to that section of the community, which we propose to term the 'social problem' or 'subnormal group'. This group comprises approximately the lowest 10 per cent of the social scale of most communities. (*Report of the Mental Deficiency Committee*, 1929: 80)

The report accepted the principally biological cause, but noted that 'low mentality and poor environment form a vicious circle' (p. 81). The eugenicists expressed themselves in stronger terms, and saw the social problem group thriving as 'some fungus thrives upon a healthy and vigorous plant' (quoted in Macnicol, 1987), and launched a series of studies to document the phenomenon. The validity of designating a social grouping on the basis of such a heterogeneous set of characteristics does not appear to have been questioned.

In 1923 the Eugenics Society (ES) set up a committee for the supervision of research into the 'social qualities and health of a sample of our population' (Macnicol, 1987: 305), with the general aim of demonstrating that destitution was a hereditary condition, which resulted in 'a group which generation after generation survives only by public support and this maintenance secures similar recurrent misery in the next generation' (ES archives, 1943, quoted in Macnicol, 1987: 306). The official support of the society was extended to Lidbetter (1933), in his documentation of the social problem group in East London. This project set out to investigate the degree of inter-generational reproduction of the pauper state, and had a particular focus on 'chargeability', i.e. receipt of public assistance. The final report testified to 'A race of sub-normal people, closely related by marriage or parenthood, not to any extent recruited from the normal population, nor sensibly diminished by agencies for social or individual improvement' (Ray, 1983: 218).

The interpretation and implications of Lidbetter's research have been ably documented by Macnicol, who makes a series of critical points. Firstly, Lidbetter noted that degeneracy could take a variety of forms, in which he included high infant mortality, blindness, insanity, and 'non-moral qualities', but all these varied forms were attributed to the same single cause of biological weakness. Secondly, despite the variation he documented among the social problem group, Lidbetter argued that there was a 'sufficiency of common characteristics such as to constitute a class by themselves'. They could, however, be divided into those showing a pronounced and obvious defect, and those showing the 'perpetuation of the merely low grade type' (1933: 18). As a profile of a homogeneous grouping this fails to convince.

Lidbetter had not been deflected from his argument by the shrinking of the pauper population with the First World War, which he interpreted as a result of lowering the standard of employable labour. The reappearance of pauperism in family histories with the recession was seen as proof of his position. Similarly, the extension of outdoor relief to the able bodied was regarded as a response to the exceptional distress caused by the industrial depression. This did not make him reflect on the validity of the concept of 'chargeability', or on the varying economic circumstances which lay behind the composition of his problem group. This same criterion of dependence was central to another study of destitution at around the same time; that of Liverpool by Caradog Jones (1934). For him the 'social problem group was defined as 'a section of the population which is largely dependent upon others for support . . . if left to themselves, many, if not the majority of them, would be in danger of destitution' (1934: 345). The concern of Caradog Jones thus returned to the assumption of biological causes of the social problem group, of whom we are exhorted to think rather 'in terms of biology than in terms of economics'. This group was elsewhere judged to be made up of those of low intelligence, or mentally defective individuals. 'Those who fail to reach a certain standard of intelligence are liable to become a social problem group, a group dependent on society by reason of the defect or disability from which they suffer' (Blacker, 1937: 225).

There were other writers, contemporary to Lidbetter and Caradog Jones, who adopted a more cautious and ambivalent approach to the linked problems of definition and explanation. Blacker (1937: 4) also writing under the auspices of the Eugenics Society but in more hesitant terms than in some of his earlier work, notes that the social problem group falls into two types: the medico-psychological, defined in terms of mental defect, and the socio-logical, defined in terms of poverty and slum dwelling. Falling somewhere between the two are the recidivists, unemployables, inebriates and prostitutes. In Blacker's work we find the clear expression of an issue contemporary to the 1990s: the failure to answer the question, 'How much unemployment is the outcome of the economic factor, lack of work, or the psychological, lack of capacity for sustained work' (1937: 7). The explanation of unemployment and consequent dependency in his argument is by no means straightforward; it may be explained by a physical or mental deficiency present at birth, or may equally affect 'a person whose past life presents no abnormally adverse features but who has nevertheless succumbed to such habits as drink, incurable laziness, quarrelsomeness, fecklessness, or to neurosis, which, when there is competition for work, cast him into unemployment and keep him there' (p. 13).

Degeneration and demoralisation were still the vital issues.

THE NEXT STEP

World war was again to challenge many of the ideas expressed above. The unemployed were once more absorbed by the demands of the war effort, whilst the impact of the war itself caused some rethinking in the area of social engineering, as did the debt of gratitude to the soldiers returning to poor conditions and a tight labour market. A Keynesian consensus of the middle way brought optimism about the possibility of non-socialist reform, which would include state intervention and economic planning in the cause of full employment. The universalism of the war effort and the educative effect of evacuation in revealing to all classes the worst effects of deprivation generated considerable concern about reconstruction. One manifestation of this was the appointment of William Beveridge to head an inquiry into the Social Insurance and Allied Services. Beveridge embarked on this task with the view that a government which could abolish unemployment in times of war could do so in times of peace. A new era of social awareness and optimism was to emerge.

This is not to say that concerns about the social problem group were finally laid to rest, but they were to emerge in a somewhat different form. The eugenic flavour of debate was certainly in decline, and the focus of interest came to be cultural rather than biological. This shift is reflected in ideas such as the cycles of deprivation of 1960s Britain, and the 'culture of poverty' debate in 1960s America, itself recycled as the 1980s 'culture of dependency'.

Before tracing the roots of these ideas, and their contemporary expression, we turn back to history, to the policy debates of the nineteenth and early twentieth centuries, and the early emergence of the promise of social citizenship; a concept apparently at odds with the existence of an underclass.

NOTES

1 The following quotations are taken from Karl Marx and Frederick Engels *Selected Works*, Vol. 1, 1951.
   (a) Prefatory note to 'The peasant war in Germany' (p. 584);
   (b) *Manifesto of the Communist Party* (p. 42);
   (c) *The Class Struggle in France* (p. 142);
   (d) *The Eighteenth Brumaire of Louis Bonaparte* (p. 267).

Chapter 2

The mischievous ambiguity

The previous chapter examined images of the poor and their implicit messages about causes of poverty. These matters are necessarily linked to policy issues concerning the treatment of the poor and the degree of collective responsibility which is considered acceptable. A common view asserts that the transition into the twentieth century saw the incremental development of social responsibility for the poor, but detail of the legislation shows a perpetuation of the deserving/undeserving distinction of nineteenth-century thought, and even its exacerbation. This chapter looks more closely at poverty policy in Britain, and the question of whether the welfare state utopia was ever really delivered.

The early industrial age, with its newly created body of wage labourers gathered together in urban concentrations, and in conditions which seemed to reduce them to something less than human, brought a growing awareness of poverty as a social problem. For some, as we saw in the previous chapter, the problem was the poor themselves. Certainly the distinction between a social structural explanation of poverty and an explanation rooted in the characteristics and morality of the individual seems often to have been blurred. The legacy of Malthusianism has been described as 'a mode of thought and feeling that seemed to be intellectually irresistible and morally repulsive' (Himmelfarb, 1984: 133). What resulted were feelings of fear and condemnation, if often alongside pity.

Early equivalents of the notion of the underclass were essentially rooted in moral condemnation, and any reliance on public assistance by the able-bodied seemed to confirm this judgement. In the debate about the Poor Law Malthus stood clearly among the abolitionists, believing that man needed the spur of want to shake him from his natural idleness. The extreme view, as expressed by Carlyle, was that those who could not support themselves should be allowed to perish, and certainly not to reproduce. It was, in part, the fear of social disorder which brought the eventual assumption of responsibility for the poor by the state, and we find in the development of this provision a preview of current conceptualisations of an 'underclass'. Policy decisions, together with developing divisions in the workforce, can be seen as playing a central role in the social construction of a 'problem group', the stigmatised dependants of the state.

The numbers of people without the means of subsistence had been swelled by two processes in the sixteenth century: the system of enclosure which denied access to common land and prompted the flow to the cities, and massive price inflation (Fraser, 1986: 32). Laws against vagrancy had existed since 1388, to inhibit the mobility of labour, but when local parishes were made responsible for the destitute there was all the more reason to oppose vagrancy; no parish wished to provide for any from outside its boundaries. The Poor Law Act of 1601 (the 43rd of Elizabeth), established an administrative framework whereby overseers appointed by local magistrates were empowered to levy a rate on property to make provision for the poor. The 1662 Act of Settlement ruled that a stranger could be removed within forty days of arrival in a parish, unless occupying freehold land. The parish was required to dispatch them to their place of settlement – i.e. their community of belonging – by birth, marriage or apprenticeship. The overseers, of course, did all they could to prevent paupers being charged to their parish. This desire to protect a community of interest and resources from the claims of outsiders finds a parallel in many and varied social circumstances, as some of the discussion of migration later in this book will demonstrate.

The impotent poor had already been identified as a group in need of special provisions, and in 1536 parishes were authorised to collect money for their support. It became increasingly necessary, in the eyes of the Poor Law Guardians, to distinguish between the genuinely destitute and the idler. The concept of setting the poor to work was established in the legislation of 1576, and the 43rd of Elizabeth introduced a system of classification: the impotent poor, the able-bodied poor, and the thriftless who required correction. For the able-bodied, relief was dependent upon their being set to work, and there was punishment for absconders. The idea of a poorhouse or workhouse was introduced at this time, to provide care for the elderly and infirm, and work for the able-bodied. Conditions in these institutions deterred all but the most desperate from entering. A nationwide network of workhouses did not exist until about 1850, and out relief was always the main form of aid. The distinction between the labouring poor and the dependent pauper was blurred by a system of subsidies (the Speenhamland system) introduced to offset the insufficiency of wages in the face of rising prices.

By the beginning of the nineteenth century, the inadequacy of the system of relief, together with the increasing burden on local rates, prompted the appointment in 1832 of a Royal Commission. Charged with inquiring into the administration of the Poor Laws, the Commission complained about the 'mischievous ambiguity' of the notion of poverty. Driven by the compulsion to seek out the deserving from the undeserving poor, society was confronted with a problem identified by de Tocqueville in his visit to England in 1833. 'Nothing is so difficult to distinguish as the nuances which separate unmerited misfortune from an adversity produced by vice.' At the root of this problem was an issue of morality, closely linked with the work ethic and the desire to maintain the incentive to work. Whilst there was no objection to providing some minimal support for the impotent (i.e. those unable to work), the main difficulties arose in the treatment of the able-bodied poor, expressed in the principle of 'less eligibility'.

Himmelfarb (1984: 163) sees this principle as based on a distinction between the pauper – a person without the means of subsistence – and the poor, who may well be gainfully employed. 'The principle of less eligibility, by making relief more meager and more onerous than the rewards of labour, kept the "pauper class" in its "proper position" below that of the "lowest class" of independent labourer' (p. 164). For as long as this requirement endured, some degree of moral blame would attach to the able-bodied unemployed, and this sentiment is reflected in de Tocqueville's critique of the right of the poor to public relief. 'What is the achievement of this right if not a notarized manifestation of misery, of weakness, of misconduct on the part of its recipient?' (quoted in Himmelfarb, 1984: 147). Part of the process of thus distinguishing the pauper from the poor was the denial of relief to those engaged in full time work. What emerged in the 1834 legislation were the three planks of the New Poor

Law: less eligibility, the workhouse test, and centralised state administration.

The premise upon which the new arrangements were based was the natural idleness of man, and their intention was to discourage pauperism, with the workhouse as the deterrent. This policy was behind the pace of change. Enough places could not be found to accommodate the fluctuating demands for labour in the urban industrial centres, and indoor relief for paupers between 1840 and 1870 never rose above 16 per cent (Fraser, 1986: 52). Poor relief, however, carried an inevitable stigma, and was to be avoided wherever possible, at a time when the individualism of classical economics and the related doctrine of self-help were taking hold. 'The Poor Law was saddled with the paradoxical aim of alienating its potential clientele and the stigma of pauperism induced a reluctance to seek official relief which became firmly rooted in popular culture' (Fraser, 1986: 55). Pauperism was seen by implication as a wilful choice of the idle, who were to be denied community membership not just by physical removal to the workhouse, but also by moral condemnation. Not surprisingly, those more securely placed in the labour market began to make their own provision for periods of short term unemployment.

THE SOCIAL DIVISION OF WELFARE

This process was one manifestation of what Mann (1986) describes as the making of a claiming class. In this argument Mann criticises a view of the working class as a homogeneous social group and moves towards a focus on the nature of inequalities and divisions within this class. Thus, 'The labour aristocracy sought not to join the middle class but to escape the grinding poverty and degradation imposed upon the working class' (p. 66). The Poor Law of 1834 was instrumental in this process, with the discipline of the workhouse and the principle of less eligibility serving to encourage workers to make provision for themselves. The Friendly Societies, from which the more vulnerable members of the working class were often excluded, were the principal means of so doing. Divisions of this kind existed even prior to industrialisation in the form of the guilds and the tramping system. The guilds were trade organisations for craftsmen, and most of them provided some kind of welfare system, whilst the tramping system offered support to facilitate the mobility of skilled labour. Both served an elite section of the workforce, and were in some senses the forerunners of the Friendly Societies.

By a system of social closure particular groups within the workforce established a monopoly of knowledge pertaining to a specific aspect of the labour process. This organisation of workers by virtue of their exclusive claims to skill contributes to the creation of a 'lesser' category of unskilled, lacking the means to strengthen their position in the labour market, and because of their vulnerability condemned to a stigmatising form of support in periods of economic decline. 'By 1872 Friendly Societies are estimated to have had over 4 million members. Only a minority of these were unskilled labourers and, for the poorest stratum of the working class, Friendly Society membership was not a realistic alternative to the poor law' (Mann, 1992: 47).

Divisions within the working class and in the nature of welfare provision were in some ways recreated in the first system of insurance against unemployment. This is perhaps surprising given the emphasis on rights earned by virtue of the contributions of the insured worker, but the system introduced in 1911 was 'a remedy for fluctuation in employment, not for unemployment' (Stevenson, 1934: 188). Provision was selective, covering only seven trades prone to seasonal or cyclical fluctuations, and was based on a treatment of unemployment as a transitory phenomenon, failing to offer provision for the long term unemployed, who were the most in need. In fact the problem underlying the insurance principle generally is that financial viability depends upon the exclusion of those most likely to place a high demand on the system.

Whilst no enquiry was made into the financial circumstances or the moral character of those claiming the benefit, a fear of abuse was evident in the restriction of benefits in proportion to contributions, the requirement of 26 weeks' contributions in order to qualify, and the maximum 15 weeks of benefit permissible in any one year. 'Armed with this double weapon of a maximum limit to benefit and of a minimum contribution, the operation of the scheme itself will automatically exclude the loafer' (Llewellyn-Smith, 1910: 507). The loafers, it was argued, would be betrayed by their record of contributions. The deserving and undeserving distinction also surfaces in the clauses concerning those who lose employment through 'misconduct', or leave a job 'without just cause'. Such workers could be denied benefit for a period of up to six weeks, despite Churchill's distaste, as President of the Board of Trade, for mixing 'moralities and mathematics'; the right to unemployment insurance was conditional on good behaviour.

The scheme was extended in 1916 to include those industries expanded because of the war, which were likely to be vulnerable to unemployment once it ended, though not without protest from the workers about the payment of contributions. Confidence in the scheme was such as to warrant its further extension to all manual workers, and to non-manual workers earning less than £250 p.a., in 1920. But the argument that the undeserving could be automatically separated out by their employment record was to be dramatically challenged by the mass unemployment of the postwar depression, and so too was the financial viability of the scheme.

At the end of the war an 'out of work donation' was introduced; a non-contributory benefit paid to ex-servicemen and civilians alike, and a first sign of things to come. Unemployment reached 18 per cent by the middle of 1921, and the number unemployed was not to fall below a million for almost twenty years (Deacon, 1976: 15). These conditions produced a population of workers who were technically insurable but who had made insufficient contributions for the receipt of benefit. Fear of social disorder, guilt about those who had fought for their country, and a reluctance to return to the Poor Law prompted the extension of the insurance scheme to 'uncovenanted workers' but also ushered in the 'search for the scrounger' (Deacon, 1976).

The ratio of benefit to contributions in the new act was one in six, 'an automatic check upon the benefit claims of a somewhat shiftless class of the community' (Watson, the government actuary, quoted in Deacon, 1976: 14). The undeserving poor were back, and, as in the above comment, seen as a distinctive 'class' of people. Further assurances against abuse were felt to be necessary to deal with uncovenanted claims, and came in the form of the 'genuinely seeking work test' for claimants without rights by virtue of contributions (introduced in March 1921). So whilst the passage from the nineteenth to the twentieth century has conventionally been seen, with regard to the poor, as a move from moral blame to collective social responsibility, in practice this transition was never fully achieved.

THE RETURN OF THE UNDESERVING POOR

Applicants for uncovenanted benefit were thus required to prove that they were 'genuinely seeking whole-time employment but unable to obtain such employment', and soon after the requirement was extended to those claiming covenanted benefit but having paid less than twenty contributions in the year preceding their claim. There had already existed a 'capable and available' requirement, but the new clause shifted the onus of proof away from the Labour Exchange, which previously had been expected to offer a job or demonstrate the availability of employment. It was felt that the flow of information about vacancies was not guaranteed, especially in the 'unorganised' (non-unionised and predominantly unskilled) industries, so there was an insufficient safeguard against the malingerer. Documentary evidence of job search by claimants offered a solution.

In February 1922 the right of uncovenanted claimants to hold out for employment equivalent to their previous position was removed and they were required to accept any work which they were reasonably capable of performing. The fact that some claimants were deemed capable of work but unwilling required a judgement on 'the state of the applicant's mind', and married women came in for particular attention. The general suspicions surrounding claimants, especially those with insufficient contributions for insurance benefit, also brought the imposition, in 1922, of a means test for uncovenanted claimants. In 1924 the 'genuinely seeking work' test was extended (by a Labour government) to cover all applications for benefit, and extra conditions were imposed on those whose credit by contribution had been exhausted.

The concerns of the period are reflected in the Report of the Unemployment Insurance Committee in 1927 (the Blanesburgh Report), which recommended a reduction of benefits for 18–21-year-olds to deter idlers, and asserted the following three conditions for benefit:

1 30 contributions in the previous two years;
2 Genuinely seeking work, and capable and available;
3 Disqualification for voluntary unemployment.

The most contentious of these was the 'genuinely seeking work' test, but the three conditions nevertheless passed into law under the then Liberal government. All claimants now had to prove their genuine search for work, and this test resolved itself into a test of character: 'It was frequently alleged that the interviews penalised the honest but nervous claimant, while allowing the confident malingerer to proceed to benefit' (Deacon, 1976: 59). Hence the judgement of the ultimate authority on appeals, the Umpire, was that 'The facts become immaterial, the capacity to tell a tale, remember it, and stick to it becomes the stuff of the decision.' Those refused benefit took recourse to the Poor Law, and were often granted outdoor relief. If not they depended upon informal support from kin and friends.

When the Labour government assumed office in 1929 a small committee was appointed to review the claims procedure, with the focus mainly on the 'seeking work' test. The argument against the test was that it should first be incumbent upon the Labour Exchange to show both that work was available, and that the claimant had some chance of obtaining it should he/she apply. This argument eventually won through and the test was abolished in March 1930. Under the amended bill a claimant would only be disallowed as not seeking work if he/she refused an offer of suitable employment or failed to carry out the instructions of an insurance officer.

That same year, only three years after the legislation of 1927, a Royal Commission was appointed to report to the new Labour government. There was increasing support at this time for the view that relief should be separated from insurance, though with differing opinions as to how this was to be achieved. One possibility was to keep the existing system intact, but remove the costs of the non-insured to the Exchequer. Others argued for some test to 'weed out' the 'flotsam and jetsam' (Deacon, 1976: 76). When the Royal Commission reported, it was to recommend a formalisation of the distinction between covenanted and uncovenanted benefit by completely removing the problem of long term unemployment from the insurance scheme. A means test for the non-insured was rejected, but concern was directed at the anomalous cases of seasonal workers and married women. The final report of the Commission was made to a national government which had already cut relief scales by 10 per cent, increased contributions and imposed a means test on benefits for the uninsured.

The legislation which followed the report, the Unemployment

Insurance Act of 1934, identified three categories of the unemployed:

1 Those entitled to benefit by virtue of their contribution record;
2 Those capable of and available for work whose entitlement to benefit had been exhausted;
3 Those no longer active in the labour market.

The first group were the responsibility of the Unemployment Insurance Statutory Committee, the second became the responsibility of the Unemployment Board, and the third remained under Public Assistance. This was a desperate measure to rescue the insurance fund from massive debt, and was in may ways the foundation of our existing system of income support: 'Suddenly the gap appeared between social justice and fiscal responsibility. What the government could afford according to the accepted economic tenets and what the working population needed in order to keep alive could not be reconciled in financial terms' (Gilbert, 1966: 168).

AN ALTERNATIVE VIEW

Whilst the main motivation for this separation had been to rescue the financial viability of the insurance fund the effect was to establish two classes of the unemployed, and to place the uninsured in danger of stigmatisation and moral condemnation. The 'out of work donation' had been introduced at the end of the First World War in recognition of the war effort and to protect of the dignity of the recipients. Political citizenship had at last been fully conceded in 1918, but exclusion from the economic life of the country was to follow for quite some time:

> The terms of exclusion of the poor from society were redefined to meet the conventions of the modern state. In place of disenfranchisement and the workhouse, there was the means test and the inspecting officer policing the management of the family economy. In theory, the bureaucratisation of welfare promoted access and justice, in practice it engendered alienation and fear. (Vincent, 1991:101)

These dangers had been identified even at the time, in the form of the Minority Report (Royal Commission, 1932), which began with the rejection of the division of the unemployed into two classes, and challenged the validity of the notion of insurance against unemployment: the risk was impossible to calculate, and placing a limit on the duration of benefit was to withdraw support just when it was most needed. Thus the imposition of a rigid ratio of benefit to contribution in times of poor trade brings 'to an abrupt and arbitrary conclusion' the benefit of otherwise genuine claimants. The consequent division of the unemployed into two groups was not in accordance with their 'personal characteristics' with regard to willingness to work, but placed a mixture of types on either side of an arbitrary line.

The validity of this line was questioned in view of the assertion that 'There is no evidence that the loss of income and less attractive conditions to which large numbers of the unemployed have been subjected . . . have resulted in any increase in the numbers obtaining work' (Royal Commission, 1932: 398). This argument was supported by evidence of sharp regional differences in employment and unemployment, which could not be said to derive from the 'mental or moral characteristics' of people in specific areas or industries. It was argued in a statement against the social division of welfare that the only satisfactory provision was through an all-inclusive scheme, 'because all occupations are interdependent, and none is self-contained or self-sufficing. The sheltered trades would not exist if it were not for the existence of the unsheltered ones' (ibid., 1932: 404).

World war for the second time solved the crisis of unemployment, and the insurance fund gradually returned to solvency. However, the universalism of the war effort, together with the educative effect of evacuation in revealing 'to the whole people the blackspots of its social life' (Minority Report, quoted in Titmus, 1950: 516) generated considerable concern about reconstruction. *The Times*, in July 1940, reported: 'The European house cannot be put in order unless we put our own house in order first. The new order cannot be based on the preservation of privilege, whether the privilege be that of a country, or a class, or of an individual.'

One manifestation of concern was the government's appointment in 1941 of William Beveridge to head an inquiry into Social Insurance and Allied Services. Beveridge's recommendations were in tune with the position of the Minority Report of some ten years earlier in that he argued for flat-rate benefit sufficient for subsistence, without a means test, to be paid for as long as unemployment lasted. The principle of the scheme was to be a pooling of risk so that the fortunate shared the cost of supporting the less fortunate. Concern with the principle of less eligibility survived, however, and led to the introduction of the Family Allowance as a universal benefit in 1945. This was intended, in part, to offset the additional allowances for the dependants of the unemployed which might raise their income above that of the lowest paid.

The major recommendations of the Beveridge Report cut across the divisions in access to welfare which were beginning to develop, asserting collective responsibility for the unemployed, and favouring equalised treatment. However, the subsequent National Insurance Act of 1946 departed from the Beveridge plan in some vital respects; notably an unlimited benefit was rejected in preference for a maximum of 30 weeks, as provision of indefinite support was reckoned to be open to abuse. The 1948 National Assistance Act finally abolished the Poor Law and established the National Assistance Board for the centralised administration of relief. This provision was predominantly concerned with the plight of the elderly and little attention was given to the others who would fall under its remit: the unemployed without insurance benefit, and the insured unemployed who required a supplement to their income. The growth of dependence on this particular form of relief as the duration of unemployment lengthened was not foreseen.

The unemployed claiming National Assistance (NA) were subject to a means test, and in theory this would seem to re-establish the deserving/undeserving distinction. In practice, because the NA rates had been set more recently than the insurance rates, the possibility was open for the insured unemployed to make application themselves, which would of course subject *them* to a means test. By the end of 1948 three-quarters of all NA claimants were in receipt of inadequate insurance benefits (Walker, 1983: 17). The objectives of abolishing poverty, providing benefit as of right, and standardising treatment were undermined from the start. Ironically, it was one of the guarantees of individual freedom which prevented the inadequacies of benefit levels from becoming apparent: there was never any precise specification of expected spending patterns. The feasibility of guaranteeing social rights to secure social citizenship for all was to become a matter of the moment.

SOCIAL CITIZENSHIP

In 1873 Alfred Marshall had written: 'The question is not whether all men will ultimately be equal . . . but whether progress may go on steadily, if slowly, till, by occupation at least, every man is a gentleman', and of the working classes, that they were 'steadily accepting the private and the public duties of a citizen'. T.H. Marshall, writing in 1950, took up these ideas, substituting the word 'gentleman' with the word 'civilised', and translating this as 'a claim to be accepted as full members of the society, that is, as citizens' (1950: 8). Such full membership of a community, he argued, was not inconsistent with the inequalities of social class, provided equality of citizenship was recognised. He is here implicitly distinguishing between a class position and a status. The Beveridge plan was arguably an attempt to guarantee such a status by virtue of the right to benefit, the assurance of subsistence, and the respect of individual autonomy. For T.H. Marshall, 'The basic human equality of membership . . . [had] been enriched with new substance and invested with a formidable array of rights. . . . It [had] been clearly identified with the status of citizenship.' He set himself to answer the question: 'Is it still true that the basic equality, when enriched in substance and embodied in the formal rights of citizenship, is consistent with the inequalities of social class?'

Marshall divides citizenship into three parts: civil, political and social. The first of these parts refers to equality before the law, the second to equal rights of participation in the political process, and the third to: 'The whole range from the right to a modicum of economic welfare and security to the right to share to the full in the social heritage and to live the life of a civilised being according to the standards prevailing in society' (1950: 11).

The formative period of each of these three rights of citizenship, Marshall argued, could be assigned to a different century: civil rights to the eighteenth century, political rights to the nineteenth, and social rights to the twentieth. The introduction of insurance-based benefits may be viewed as a clear example of this development. Marshall sees the beginning of social rights in the 'local communities and functional associations' which were gradually replaced by the Poor Law, and by wage regulation, and later wage supplements (the Speenhamland system). Here the drive for social rights was felt to be in competition with civil rights, and notably the free operation of the market. In this it was doomed to failure, he argues, 'because it was utterly obnoxious to the prevailing spirit of the times' (p. 23).

Social rights lost the battle in so far as the minimum social rights that were granted were detached from the status of citizenship:

> The Poor Law treated the claims of the poor not as an integral part of the rights of the citizen, but as an alternative to them . . . paupers forfeited in practice the civil right of personal liberty, by internment in the workhouse, and they forfeited by law any political rights they might possess. (p. 24)

Nor was this policy so distant from the mood at the turn of the century. In 1906 Beveridge had argued that the 'unemployable' 'Must become the acknowledged dependants of the state . . . but with a complete and permanent loss of all citizen rights including not only the franchise but civil freedom and fatherhood' (1906: 327).

Traditionally, the very receipt of assistance had been a denial of citizenship and implied a separation from 'the community' and a passage to the status of 'outcast'. Marshall is principally interested in whether the inequalities generated by capitalism can ever be reconciled with the equality implicit in citizenship. He argues that in a class system based on status, in which different rights and duties attach to different positions, as in medieval feudalism, equality cannot be achieved through the guarantee of social citizenship. The same is not felt to be true of a class system based on acheived standards of living, where the difference between class positions is quantitative, not qualitative. 'The working classes, instead of inheriting a distinctive though simple culture, are provided with a cheap and shoddy imitation of a civilisation which has become national' (Marshall, 1950: 31). In this situation, he states, the inequality reflected in class distinctions can be ameliorated without challenge to the basic principles of the system.

The move from status to contract which came with the transition to capitalism in principle laid the responsibility of self-maintenance on every 'citizen', but accorded the civil rights of freedom and equality in the market. Social rights do undermine the implied obligation of the citizen to be self-reliant, states Marshall, but do not *necessarily* undermine the operation of the free market and its associated system of inequality. His argument is that civil rights became a vehicle for workers to establish entitlement to certain social rights: 'These aspirations have in part been met by incorporating social rights into the status of citizenship and thus creating a universal right to real income which is not proportionate to the market value of the claimant' (p. 47). The history of British social policy shows the development of social rights emerging from a genuine sense of national community which resulted from the efforts of the Second World War, the sense of debt owed to common soldiers, and to some extent the fear of their political power.

The degree of equalisation achieved by such rights depends, according to Marshall, on four things: 'Whether the benefit is offered to all or to a limited class; whether it takes the form of money payment or service rendered; whether the minimum is high or low; and how the money to pay for the benefit is raised' (p. 54). Benefit which is means tested is argued to offer abatement of class inequalities, but in a selective manner, so that only the genuinely needy benefit. The drawback is that 'economic equalisation might be accompanied by psychological class discrimination' because of the stigma attached to pauper status. Insurance benefit removes the means test, and makes a bigger percentage addition to small incomes than to large. The main achievement of this and other services however is argued to lie in the reduction of risk and insecurity. In this sense, 'Equalisation is not so much between classes as between individuals within a population which is now treated for this purpose as though it were one class. Equality of status is more important than equality of income' (p. 56).

But the benefit itself may operate as an instrument of social stratification, argues Marshall. The example he gives is the education system, which provides a service according to class position, and by virtue of the differential quality of the service, class positions are reproduced. These arguments have been expressed more fully with reference to the whole welfare system by Titmus (1958), and later developed by Sinfield (1978). In the social insurance and public assistance of the 1940s, however, it may be argued that despite its promise the nature of the provision may have offset some material inequality yet created differences of status which are still with us. Marshall accepts such a possibility (albeit with reference to education and occupation), but argues: that 'Status differences can receive the stamp of legitimacy in terms of democratic citizenship provided they do not cut too deep, but occur within a population united in a single civilization' (p. 75).

Can this be said of the system of benefit which emerged from the Beveridge plan?

BEVERIDGE AND AFTER

With the Beveridge plan social citizenship must have seemed to have arrived, attacking the five giants of Want, Disease, Ignorance, Squalor and Idleness. We have been principally concerned with the first and the last of these, and certainly 'Want' was to be taken care of by the National Insurance and National Assistance Acts discussed above. National Insurance embodied the ideal of support in need as of right, and the right was won by contributory payments. In this way the obligation of responsibility for self is upheld, the rules of participation are universally applied, and equality of status is guaranteed. The debatable point is whether the claimant was assured, in the words of T.H. Marshall, 'the right to share to the full in the social heritage and to live the life of a civilised being according to the standards prevailing in society' (1950: 11). On the answer to this question turn a number of other issues.

One of the most important features of the Beveridge Report was the recommendation to set benefits at subsistence level. However, although Beveridge argued in favour of subsistence provision he was also concerned with the financial soundness of the scheme and with the need for an incentive to seek employment; both considerations pointed towards a minimal benefit. He consequently adopted a most stringent definition of subsistence. Although he consulted a number of authorities on basic needs (see Dilnot *et al.*, 1984: 34) and was strongly influenced by Rowntree's research into poverty in York (1941), Beveridge set a level at 1938 prices which was only about two-thirds of the Rowntree poverty line. This was principally because the Beveridge line contained no allowance for expenditure other than on food, clothing and fuel, whilst Rowntree had included a number of other personal and household items. The problem of adequacy was worsened by two other factors.

The White Paper which followed the Beveridge Report accepted many of its suggestions, but the subsistence basis was deemed impracticable; a high level of benefit would mean a level of contribution which was possibly higher than 'the great body of contributors could be properly asked to bear'. By the time the legislation went through parliament inflation had anyway outdated Beveridge's calculations, and in order to offset this rise an addition of 31 per cent was made to the sums originally set out on the basis of 1938 prices. The adequacy of this concession has ever since been in contention. 'The awkward fact, not mentioned by any of the Labour ministers responsible, was that the cost of living at the end of 1945 was already 45 per cent higher than in 1938' (Kincaid, 1973: 59).

The immediate question this raises is the adequacy of the insurance benefit, and the level of income necessary in order to 'share to the full in the social heritage'. Another is the relation of insurance benefit to the means tested National Assistance (NA), and its implications for rights of social inclusion. Despite the questionable adequacy of the insurance benefit with reference to Rowntree's, and even Beveridge's calculations, comparisons made in 1946 between the proposed scale and the old Assistance scale (unchanged since 1944) reflected well on the insurance rates, which were heralded as a 'virtual abolition of the means test' (Deacon, 1982: 299). However, when the new National Assistance scales came to be set in 1948 there had been a further rise of 8 per cent in the cost of living index, and as a result the NA rates were set rather higher than the 1946 insurance rates. This raised the possibility of supplementation of insurance benefits with NA, and with it the quick return of means testing. As we have seen, by 1949 a majority of NA claims were supplementing inadequate insurance benefits and pensions. A failure of both scales was the decision not to grant the full subsistence rates for children, in addition to which adult rates were based on the needs of pensioners, despite advice that the needs of people of working age would be greater.

The pattern of supplementary claims for NA, together with the decision that insurance benefit should be of limited duration, exposed many unemployed claimants to a means test. The ideal of social citizenship guaranteed by state welfare provisions is necessarily damaged by this development, first because it introduces differences of status within the welfare system, and secondly because it imposes conditions other than the lack of employment on the receipt of benefit. Where benefit is as of right by virtue of contributions the possibility of social stigma is reduced, but the more conditions which are attached to a claim the more damage is done to the self-esteem and public status of the claimant. It is thus that a system which seemed to offer the guarantee of social citizenship at its inception has been transformed into a system which is associated with the designation 'underclass' (e.g. Runciman, 1990), and with social, if not political disenfranchisement.

ADEQUACY AND SOCIAL INCLUSION

In the early years of National Assistance, upgradings were intended to do no more than compensate for rising prices. During the 1950s there was an attempt to extend the increasing affluence of society to the recipients of welfare, which was largely frustrated by inflation (SBC, 1977). In 1966 National Assistance was replaced by Supplementary Benefit (SB), with short term rates set slightly below National Insurance (NI) benefit levels, and long term rates slightly higher than the NI pension rate. The unemployed were specifically excluded from receipt of this long term rate, which was anyway abolished with the introduction of Income Support in 1988, to be replaced with a system of premiums. A procedure was established whereby the short term rate was upgraded with reference to prices, and the long term rate with reference to wages, with the effect that the unemployed, who were confined to the short term rate, were not accorded the same proportional income increases as those in work (where the rate of the increase exceeded inflation). So within the safety net system of SB the unemployed were discriminated against, presumably with a view to protecting the principle of 'less eligibility'. The premiums introduced in 1988 now include the unemployed with families, but the childless unemployed remain disadvantaged in relation to other groups.

The benefit level for the unemployed has hovered between 40 and 50 per cent of the net manual wage, and in the high unemployment years of the 1980s only about a quarter of unemployed claimants existed solely on claims for the NI benefit (i.e Unemployment Benefit). There have been a number of changes in the system in recent years, but their impact on the circumstances of the unemployed has been expressed as follows: 'The great majority [of changes] have made the system less gene-rous and have weakened the role of unemployment insurance as opposed to unemployment assistance' (Atkinson and Micklewright, 1989: 17–18). In other words, there has been a move away from contributory benefit paid as of right, towards means tested benefit for which eligibility must be assessed. These details have important implications for notions of social citizenship; 'the right to share to the full in the social heritage and to live the life of a civilised being according to the standards prevailing in society' (Marshall, 1950: 11). What proportion of average income guarantees such partici- pation? Not surprisingly, much of the debate about adequacy of benefit rates has been in terms not of 'citizenship' but of 'poverty', though both of these concepts can carry some sense of minimal social inclusion.

Setting a rate for benefit might be seen as a public statement about what are considered to be the minimum needs of particular population groups, at particular moments in time, in a particular society. Even this assumption is contentious, and John Moore, as Minister of Social Security has argued: 'you end up measuring poverty by the means used to prevent it. . . . Then increasing benefit actually increases poverty' (Moore, 1989). If we accept that a level of resources below this official minimum implies poverty, then the exercise of setting a benefit rate involves us immediately in the debate about how poverty should be defined. This debate has revolved around a fundamental distinction between relative and absolute poverty. Absolute poverty is defined with reference to the minimum income necessary for physical efficiency, and even to establish this amount is by no means straightforward. There is now, however, a general acceptance of the fact that ideas about what constitutes poverty are in essence judgements affected by what is considered to be reasonable in any given society. They are in this sense relative to the generally accepted standard of living in that society (cf. Marshall's social citizenship).

Mack and Lansley (1984) define poverty as 'an enforced lack of socially perceived necessities', while Townsend (1979) operates with the notion of participation, which includes fulfilling the normal social obligations of friendship, parenthood, etc., and involvement in generally accepted public celebrations, such as Christmas. Establishing quite what 'participation' means is far from straightforward in a society in which, to quote Townsend and Gordon (1989), 'if the richest 20% were to be denied only one eighth of their disposable incomes . . . the incomes of the poorest 20% could in theory be more than doubled'. The decision on where to draw the poverty line is a matter of judgement, and as a result has been termed 'subjective'. In fact a 'subjective' definition of poverty would be one which relied on people's own judgements about whether or not they felt poor, and this is a different matter from arguing that it is possible to arrive at some statement of what constitutes a 'reasonable standard of living' in a given society. There is a wealth of data available which illustrates in different ways a finding summed up by Bradshaw and Morgan (1987: 13): 'By the standards of living of most families today, the evidence reveals that families on Supplementary Benefit can only afford an extremely drab and restricted lifestyle.' Does this constitute the 'full membership of society' envisaged by Marshall as the basis of social citizenship, or are there reasons to justify the denial of such membership to some of the population?

CONDITIONAL RIGHTS

For Marshall the social rights which comprise social citizenship 'imply an absolute right to a certain standard of civilization which is conditional only on the discharge of the general duties of citizenship' (1950: 94). We have seen already that problems attach to the practical task of setting the standard in material terms. Further problems arise in connection with the duties owed by a citizen, some of which are at odds with the operation of welfare. There are a number of means through which claimants may demonstrate that they are deserving of benefit; one is submission to a means test to prove need. The test in itself is commonly regarded as stigmatising, as is subsequent receipt of the benefit. Barbalet (1988: 66) is correct to argue that:

> It is likely that those most in need of social services are least likely to receive them as rights properly understood. Social rights and social policy are analytically quite distinct, and the empirical relationship between the two is quite distinct.

According to Barbalet, social rights can at best be used as a rod against which social policy can be measured, by asking how far policies secure rights. No concrete examples are given, but there can, for example, be a right to benefit, though that right may be attached to conditions which undermine other social rights, or which inhibit full social inclusion.

Much public debate about the causes of unemployment, and more generally the public images of the unemployed, is still shaped by notions of a deserving and undeserving poor. A tension which has been present from the inception of public assistance of any kind has been the potential conflict between the wish to provide for maintenance and the fear of undermining the work incentive. Ironically, this fear seems to grow as unemployment itself is rising. Thus, there is a tendency to seek an explanation for high or rising levels of unemployment in the attitude of those most affected. There is also a tendency to doubt the validity of their claims. Fears of fraud and abuse undermine the social rights embodied in welfare, and tighten up the requirement to demonstrate both need and a genuine willingness to work.

Along with suspicions that those claiming unemployment benefit are secretly holding down jobs exist contrasting fears that that they are work-shy and therefore not really looking for employment. A check on both these possibilities comes in the requirement that to qualify for benefit the unemployed must be available for and actively seeking employment. This, it might be argued in Marshall's terms, is seen to be one of the minimal obligations of a citizen, an obligation upon which social rights will depend. However, 'unemployment is not so incontrovertible a "condition" as old age and is not so outside the control of the individual as sickness. People do sometimes give up jobs needlessly and sometimes make little effort to get work once unemployed' (Hill, 1974: 1). The right to benefit is denied people who voluntarily leave their job, and one right thus impinges upon another. Ritchie and Faulkner (1989), in a study of voluntary unemployment disqualification, found that those with only one disqualification cited working conditions or personal circumstances as reasons for leaving their jobs. Workers with two or more disqualifications also gave reasons related to the job, but more often it was the nature of the work, long and unsocial hours, or low pay. In the present British system of social security these are not sufficient reasons for the state to offer support, but are not rights to reasonable conditions of employment part of social citizenship?

The more conditions which attach to benefit the stronger the system of surveillance and the greater the impingement on individual freedom will be. Growing concern about levels of public spending throughout the 1980s in Britain prompted a tightening of procedures for claimants, by the introduction of claimant advisors with potentially conflicting responsibilities; their role is to offer counselling to claimants, but also to check their availability for work. We saw in the previous chapter that this was a contentious issue throughout the high unemployment of the 1920s. It became so again in the 1980s.

The conditions surrounding a claim were generally tightened. Specified limits were imposed on the period for which individuals may place restrictions on the kind of work they will accept; the judgement had previously been discretionary. No assurance was given that a person would not be required to accept employment paying less than the claimant would receive in benefit. Furthermore, the onus of proof of job search was once again placed more firmly on the claimant, who may now be required to show that he/she is actively seeking employment: 'Availability implies some active step by the person concerned to draw attention to *his* availability; it is not a passive state in which a person may be said to be available provided *he* is sought out and *his* location is ascertained' (Ogus and Barendt, 1988: 93). Between 1985 and 1987 the number of decisions disallowing Unemployment Benefit on the grounds of non-availability for work nearly doubled, from 53,680 to 101,774 (Hansard, 28 October 1988, col. 457).

The requirement of relentless 'active' search in circumstances under which it is unlikely to pay off has been the focus for criticism, argued to have a discouraging effect and to cause unnecessary demoralisation – here meaning loss of hope. These conditions are linked to fears of undermining the will to work, and the assumption that where a reasonable living is provided by the state then there will be some for whom this is preferable to employment (cf. Malthus). On the other hand, the right to benefit is increasingly dependent upon a discouraging, demoralising and humiliating procedure in which claimants are called upon to prove their worth. In Marshall's terms this can only be construed as one of the duties of the citizen, but drawing the line where such conditions become unreasonable is as difficult as drawing the line regarding acceptable material standards of living.

STIGMA OR CITIZENSHIP?

Of course one deterrent, if such is needed, comes in the form of the social stigma which attaches to those who are benefit dependent, especially if they are capable of work. Ironically, Golding and Middleton (1982) found that the stigma which attaches to claiming is greatest in areas of highest unemployment, reflecting a general tendency to explain unemployment by the attitudes of those affected. An associated finding was that 'benefits to meet need were only stigma free where that need had an unambiguous and socially acceptable cause' (p. 163). This is reflected in the general levels of support for different types of welfare spending. Taylor-Gooby (1986:3) states: 'What seems to emerge is a consensus on priorities in the major areas of welfare spending, coupled with a less than wholehearted support for the needs of the traditionally undeserving.'

The stigma of unemployment also seems to influence the take-up of other benefits. In-work benefits have been developed as one solution to the unemployment trap whereby wages below benefit levels were thought to deter claimants from taking employment. Proof of this point is far from conclusive (see Morris, 1991: 101–3) but in-work benefits provide a means for enhancing the income of families with children. The interesting point about the Family Credit which currently operates to this effect is the very low level of take-up, at little over 50 per cent. There have been various attempts to explain this pattern, with lack of knowledge being an obvious possibility. However, 'a number of studies have found that, although eligible non-claimants may explain their behaviour in terms of ignorance, they will fail to apply when provided with information' (Deacon and Bradshaw, 1983: 133). It has further been argued that when claimants finally reach the end of a period of unemployment they may be reluctant to embark again on the process of claiming benefit. Davies and Ritchie (1988: 76) reveal that 'an examination of the nature and basis of the major inhibiting factors suggests that they are often underpinned by negative attitudes towards the whole of income support'. This is linked to pride in being able to manage, and the high value placed on independence. 'Independence appears to be at the end of many chains of questioning, a fundamental and unquestioned value in this society' (1988: 6). Such a finding directly contradicts the growing belief that the welfare state in Britain has created a 'dependency culture' (Moore, 1989). The notion of dependence has been fundamental to definitions of 'a residual class', and this is still the case in contemporary debate.

Having its roots in individualism, the very notion of citizenship rests upon the idea of an autonomous individual exercising independence and initiative, and where necessary self-restraint. Increasingly it is being argued that the mechanisms set in place to guarantee a minimal social citizenship are undermining the individual qualities upon which the concept depends. This assumption is far from proven, and there is a strong counter-argument which sees the denial of citizenship in terms of stigma and loss of pride on the part of claimants. Barbalet (1988: 66) has related both of these issues to the practice of social policy, which may:

> undermine the qualities individuals require in order to recognize and exercise rights. This is particularly so in a welfare state where the delivery of social services is dominated by over-worked and under-staffed bureaucracies and professions which, in spite of their best intentions, tend to operate in ways which emphasize the dependent status of their clients.

Certainly a growing emphasis on fraud and abuse creates an inevitable tension between the relief of need and the detection of abuse, which is arguably damaging to the relationship between claimants and staff.

> A combination of resource constraints, staff attitudes and beliefs, and claimant tactics gives rise to practices which sustain and reproduce the categories 'deserving' and 'undeserving' at the very same time that the staff insist that such practices are actually intended to vitiate this distinction. (Howe, 1985: 49)

On the basis of observations at a local social security office in Northern Ireland, Howe argues that the practice of staff is to transfer the onus of welfare promotion to the claimant, who must know and pursue his/her entitlement. Marshall has made a related observation (1975: 207): 'The rights of citizenship are a reality only for those who have belief in their authenticity and the skills needed to exercise them.' The problems observed by Howe have been partly due to staff shortages, which have also generated tensions and increased error. Those who do relentlessly pursue their rights are labelled grasping, pushy and greedy, in short 'undeserving', whilst judgements are also made on the basis of appearance, demeanour, status, income and savings (Howe, 1985: 68): 'Local practice . . . rather than being unambiguously devoted to the promotion of claimants' welfare instead withholds information, gives practical priority to the prevention and detection of fraud and abuse, and generally impugns, by implication, the motives of most clients' (p. 65). Again, as with the Poor Law, the instrument of material relief has become the means of social stigma and exclusion, and is increasingly associated with speculation about an emergent British 'underclass'.

Chapter 3

The 'New' World

The history of the development of social welfare in the US had much in common, in the early years, with that of Britain. In fact, early provision drew to a considerable extent on the precedent of the British Poor Law. Both countries were dealing with the same social and economic transformation: from a predominantly agricultural economy to a manufacturing economy based on wage labour, with the creation in the process of a destitute population. The transition happened more rapidly in the States, and the internal situation was more complex – both administratively, and in terms of regional and ethnic variation. Many of the same debates were pursued in the US as in Britain, but the two systems of public relief which emerged differ in more than detail, and in ways that have implications both for the notion of social citizenship and for the concept of the underclass.

Colonial America was a land of promise, with abundant resources, sparse population, and a liberal system of land tenure. Piven and Cloward (1971: 46) argue that such factors 'helped to nurture the strident American belief in individualism – the unshakable conviction held by poor and affluent alike that rags could indeed be converted to riches'. The problem of dependency is an inevitable part of social life, however, by virtue of age and disability, and in addition many early immigrants arrived in the New World in no condition to exploit its opportunities. The isolation and self-reliance of many of the early settlements produced an informal system of mutual support, but eventually a more formalised system of relief was needed. A sense of mutual obligation, rooted in religion and expressed through local responsibility was a strong feature of early provisions based on a local tax. 'The most common seventeenth century practice . . . was to place the poor in private homes at public expense' (Trattner, 1984: 19). This was sometimes a means of subsidising support within the extended family, and often viewed as an 'outrageous abuse of the taxpayer' (Katz, 1986: 19). More commonly, poor people were auctioned off to whoever could offer the lowest cost of maintenance, often to be treated with 'barbarity and neglect' (Yates Report, 1824).

As in Britain, the local basis for relief was a predictable source of tension. Communal responsibility was not extended readily to outsiders, and by the mid-seventeenth century restrictions had been placed on immigration and the mobility of strangers. The question of boundaries of responsibility and definitions of community membership thus represent the first problems for any system of public relief. Trattner (1984: 22) cites some instances of this problem in practice: masters of vessels bringing immigrants were required to post a bond for passengers and crew who might become a public charge, while refugees from frontier wars were often 'warned away'. Many communities established residency requirements for eligibility for public assistance, a parallel to the English Settlement and Removal Act of 1662. Concern about the drain on local resources led to the first centralised provision, in 1701, whereby the colonial treasury reimbursed local communities for unsettled persons with contagious diseases who could not be moved on. The idle stranger was excluded from membership of the 'community', while a different kind of exclusion applied to strangers by race; both blacks and Indians were deemed inferior and uncivilised, and denied any claim on public responsibility.

The strength of Calvinism and the Protestant work ethic ensured a view of voluntary idleness as vice, and as a threat to the prosperity of the community. Again as in Britain, the able-bodied poor were objects of suspicion and also as in England from the mid-seventeenth century (Katz, 1986: 14), poorhouses were established as a means of discipline and relief, growing in numbers throughout the eighteenth century. By the end of the seventeenth century Friendly Societies and charitable organisations had developed offering some system of mutual aid for members and often offering charitable support as well. Trattner notes a challenge to Calvinist belief in predestination through the 'Great Awakening' which claimed that all could achieve salvation. The movement served to fuel philanthropy and mutual concern, but also contained the seeds of an ideology of individual responsibility. However, dependency took many forms, with widows, orphans and wounded soldiers seeking refuge from the Indian wars. There was a high rate of illegitimacy, disease was rife, and much of the available work was seasonal and poorly paid. Like England, America was confronted with the problem of classifying the poor.

The system of support was severely strained by the mechanisation of agriculture, rapid industrialisation, continuing immigration, and increasing urbanisation, especially in the East. Between 1820 and 1860 5 million immigrants entered the US, amid claims that foreign countries were dumping their poor on American shores. The Commissioners from New York City's poorhouse complained of the growing expense 'not so much from the increase of our own poor, as from the prodigious influx of indigent foreigners' (Trattner, 1984: 55). Similarly the Philadelphia Board of Guardians wrote, in 1827, 'One of the greatest burthens that falls upon this corporation, is the maintenance of the host of worthless foreigners, disgorged upon our shores' (Katz, 1986: 17).

At a time of expansion and optimism the poor became increasingly suspect; the assumption that work was available to any who would take it, and the idea of individual responsibility began to take a firmer hold. Katz (1986: 6) argues:

> The availability of work for every ablebodied person who really wants a job is one of the enduring myths of American history. In fact, work was no more universally available in the early and mid-nineteenth century than it is today, as unskilled and semi-skilled workers overstocked urban labour markets.

By the mid-nineteenth century nearly every county had its poorhouse.

THE UNDESERVING POOR

In this period the classification of the poor became paramount. The settlement system already contained within it the two categories of neighbour and stranger, and the latter was deemed undeserving of community resources. This led to a harsh and costly system of transporting the destitute, often old and/or sick, from one location to another at a time when social and economic upheaval had prompted mobility in search of work. One of the expectations of the poorhouse system was that the issue of settlement would be greatly simplified, presumably because such provision would reduce mobility, but also because mandatory work and the prohibition on alcohol would deter many potential applicants.

The objective underlying the poorhouse system was to break the link assumed to exist between public relief and idleness. As in Britain, there was growing concern about the maintenance of the work incentive, and the problem was how to sustain the needy without killing individual responsibility. The Quincy Report on American Public Relief in 1821 made the predictable distinction between the 'impotent' poor and the 'able' poor, and traced the 'evils' of the existing system to the difficulty of discriminating between the two. Thus the 'mischievous ambiguity' appeared on the other side of the Atlantic. The Yates Report, commissioned from the New York secretary of state and based on responses from Poor Law officials throughout the state concluded, in 1824: 'Our poor laws are manifestly defective in principle, and mischievous in practice, and . . . under the imposing and charitable aspect of affording relief exclusively to the poor and infirm, they frequently invite the ablebodied vagrant to partake of the same bounty.'

Yates also expressed concern for the morals and education of children born into poverty, growing up in 'filth, idleness and disease, becoming early candidates for the prison or the grave'. By this time the opposition to pauperism was firmly established, with Burroughs (1834: 3–10) distinguishing between the misfortune of 'poverty' and the 'wilful error' of pauperism, 'a misery of human creation, the pernicious work of man, the lamentable consequence of bad principles and morals'. What began as an administrative category of public dependence turned into a moral issue; what was intended initially as relief for the poor attached to them the stigma of 'pauper'.

For some, morality held the answer; since the country offered abundant opportunity and resources all that was needed were the correct habits. A number of voluntary agencies took upon themselves the task of moral improvement, akin to the 'remoralisation' attempts in England. One such was the New York Association for Improving the Condition of the Poor, created in 1843. The poorhouses similarly had an educational and moral orientation, being designed to instil improved behaviour and work habits, but again the poorhouse became one of the means of sustaining the work ethic and discouraging pauperism. These institutions were an improvement on the auctioning out of the poor, but the system produced conditions which were nevertheless a deterrent to any but the most desperate. As Katz explains (1986: 25): 'A preoccupation with order, routine and cost replaced the founders' concern with the transformation of character and social reform. Everywhere, reform gave way to custody as the basis of institutional life.' As a result, 'One lesson observers learned was the incompatibility of deterrence and compassion: the spread of fear and the kindly treatment of decent poverty could not co-exist. One or other always prevailed' (Katz, 1986: 35).

Until the 1870s the number receiving outdoor relief exceeded those in poorhouses (Katz, 1986: 37), but from the 1870s onwards the situation was reversed and indoor relief became dominant. The attack on outdoor relief, which nevertheless persisted, was motivated by fears of moral degeneration, loss of the will to work, and interference with the operation of the labour market. One effect was the break-up of families as desperate parents placed their children in institutional care. Outdoor relief was never fully abolished, but its use was severely restricted to a tightly defined category of the worthy poor. Opposition to such relief was fuelled by a religious revival in the form of the Second Great Awakening (Smith Rosenberg, 1971), which was based upon the rejection of predestination and with it the assertion of individual responsibility.

The New York Association for Improving the Condition of the Poor was concerned with the threat to social stability posed by urban poverty, and with the individual depravity which was held to be the underlying cause. The aim of the organisation was to awaken the poor to the 'flaws of character which underlay their degradation' (quoted in Boyer, 1978), and towards the end of the nineteenth century Charity Organisation Societies embracing 'scientific charity' took up the opposition to public relief. The objectives of this movement were principally moral and educational, and the aim was to challenge the assumption of relief as of right, and return to the principle of voluntaristic charity; the poor could be taught self-reliance (e.g. Lowell, 1884). The plausibility of such a position had, as Katz puts it, 'floated on nearly 15 years of prosperity'. The depression of 1893 conclusively undermined its individualistic focus.

Again as in England this apparent shift in thinking did not prevent the theories of eugenicists from taking hold, and the idea of transmitted dependency was argued by Dugdale in his famous study of the Jukes family in the 1870s (Dugdale, 1877). By the turn of the century there were campaigns for the incarceration and sterilisation of the dependent population. 'Eugenics, then, tossed the mantle of science over the ancient distinction between the worthy and the unworthy poor' (Katz, 1986: 183). The new school of thought was used not just to attack public relief, but to justify the exclusion of immigrants and the suppression of black demands with arguments about inferior genetic makeup. Although the influence of eugenics was waning by the 1930s these ideas have never definitively subsided, and are periodically revived, as we see in the next chapter.

THE SHOCK OF DEPRESSION

The worst of the depression occurred in the year 1893–4, but overall lasted until 1897. Unemployment nationally was close to 20 per cent, though as high as 40 per cent in specific areas and industries. The claims of the scientific charity movement faded in the face of data gathering which gradually established that poverty has causes above and beyond the character and capacities of the individual. This view was already taking hold before the depression, and in 1886 when Buzelle addressed a national conference of charity organisations, he stated that 'the poor . . . have not in common any type of physical, intellectual, or moral development which would warrant an attempt to group them as a class' (quoted in Trattner, 1984: 100). A study of the records of the New York Charity Organisation Society over the depression years showed lack of employment, followed by sickness and accident, to be the major cause of poverty, and Hunter's influential work *Poverty*, published in 1904, showed 10 million Americans (one in eight) to be living below the conditions for normal existence. Poverty was increasingly argued to be bred of 'conditions of work and of living which are so unjust and degrading that men are driven by them to degeneracy' (Hunter, 1904; repr. 1965: 328).

The response in terms of relief was a burst of effort by private and public agencies to provide soup kitchens, free lodging houses and public work projects, the latter also supported by private associations. The old opposition to outsiders reappeared with the growth of bands of the unemployed tramping the country in search of work. This was not, however, a problem which could be easily attributed to the flaws of the individual, and Katz (1986: 149) argues that one lasting effect of the depression was the discovery of unemployment. The system of relief had proved inadequate to deal with the problem.

Despite the depression of the 1890s the turn of the century was a period of great expansion and change with a rise in manufacturing employment from 2.7 million in 1880 to 8.4 million in 1920. This expansion was linked to urban growth, rural urban migration, and also to immigration from Europe. Municipal spending on services increased dramatically, and concern grew over the need to construct an adequate system of public relief. The aim at that stage was independence from federal government, but co-operation with both charitable and business associations. The quest for efficiency in the labour market at this time provided a fertile breeding ground for eugenics, and at times an opposition to immigration. Despite the expansive nature of this period the demand for labour was far from steady and the intermittent lay-offs left families periodically destitute.

As ever, the most vulnerable were excluded from such provision as was made for workers, and the welfare capitalism of the period had fairly limited impact. A movement for workers' insurance was founded in 1906 by a team of academics, concerned primarily with accident compensation. Insurance against unemployment was much slower in coming, and was not accepted in America until 1930, in contrast to 1911 in Britain. Like Britain, America began with a limited scheme to cover workers with hard-to-replace skills or high seniority, offered by employer sponsored funds. In most cases benefits were small and limited to ten weeks.

In August 1931 over 8 million men were unemployed (Piven and Cloward, 1971). Between 1929 and 1933 official unemployment rose from 3.2 per cent to 24.9 per cent (Katz, 1986: 207) and in many areas the rate was much higher. The need for federal relief was pressing and the division between the worthy and unworthy poor was challenged. The task of relief fell at first to private local agencies, and the suggestion of federal aid was strongly resisted by Hoover: 'I am opposed to any direct or indirect government dole. The breakdown and increased unemployment in Europe is due in part to such practices. Our people are providing against distress from unemployment in true American fashion' (Piven and Cloward, 1971: 53).

A system of federal loans to states was established under the Reconstruction Finance Corporation, but when Franklin Delano Roosevelt took office in 1932 he instituted the first ever system of federal relief, and shortly after there followed a massive public works programme. The Federal Emergency Relief Administration (FERA) operated from May 1933 until June 1936, on a system whereby grants were made to states conditional on their matching the money (one federal dollar for three state dollars). By the winter of 1934, 20 million people were on the dole, including 30 per cent of the black population (Piven and Cloward, 1971: 73, 76).

The ideals upon which Roosevelt based these decisions were collective responsibility, an acknowledgement of the social and economic forces which created unemployment, and the individual's right to an assured minimum standard of living. This notion comes close to Marshall's concept of social citizenship, and was a departure from the previously established ideology of individual responsibility. The system of work relief programmes, however, established relief as something earned rather than as unconditionally available, and this has been a principle evident in much subsequent provision for the needy. The Civil Works Administration, unlike the FERA, offered assistance which was not conditional upon a means test and did much to protect the dignity of recipients and avoid stigmatisation. When it was terminated in 1934, after some business pressure against government interference in the market, it left 4 million people without work. Within a month of this the FERA was replaced with the Emergency Relief Appropriations Act. Roosevelt had warned that:

> continued dependence on relief induces a spiritual and moral disintegration fundamentally destructive to the national fiber. To dole out relief in this way is to adminster a narcotic, a subtle destroyer of the human spirit. . . . We must preserve not only the bodies of the unemployed from destitution but also their self-respect, the self-reliance and courage and determination. (Katz, 1986: 226; Piven and Cloward, 1971: 94)

A new work programme (WPA) would assume responsibility for the employables, and the rest would be returned to responsibility at state, not federal, level.

With a view to creating something more permanent Roosevelt had set up a committee of experts to devise a system of contributory insurance in 1934, and when it reported in January 1935 it was with a programme for social security which was then transmitted to Congress to become law in August 1935 (Trattner, 1984: 271). The provision took two forms: contributory social insurance and public assistance; the former covered old age and unemployment of limited duration, and the latter categorical relief principally aimed at children in need, i.e. those lacking the support of a father, the crippled and the blind. This two-tier system of insurance and public assistance is familiar from our account of the evolution of the British system of welfare, but differs in one major respect: it offers no support for the unemployed without rights by virtue of contributions.

In practice it ushered back in the distinction between the deserving and the undeserving poor. It has also been criticised for neglect of the permanently disabled and seasonal and domestic workers, and its failure to cater for a system of health insurance. For this reason Katz (1986) describes the American system as a 'semi-welfare state'. Unemployment insurance is designed to pay for itself, though we saw the problems which ensued from this assumption in Britain. It may also, as in the States, reflect established inequalities by linking benefit to wage levels. It is acceptable because it is believed to be earned, and by implication stigmatises other forms of relief which are not. Katz's conclusion on the achievements of social security states:

> It modified but did not erase archaic distinctions between the worthy and unworthy or the able bodied and impotent poor; it created walls between social insurance and public assistance that preserved class distinctions and reinforced the stigma attached to relief or welfare; in no way did it redistribute income or interfere with welfare's role in the regulation of the labour market and the preservation of social order. (1986: 247)

AID TO FAMILIES WITH DEPENDENT CHILDREN

The apparently insignificant provision for needy children, in the form of Aid to Families with Dependent Children (AFDC), was to become the basis for a welfare explosion in the 1960s, and the contentious focus for much of the subsequent 'underclass' debate. Intended as a provision for widows it has become a principal means of support for large numbers of single mothers, whose plight has been linked by many to the non-viability of the breadwinner role for many men, particularly black men. In 1961 the Social Security Act was amended to permit the inclusion of families with unemployed fathers in AFDC provision, but as of 1969 only 24 states had taken up this option, and with eligibility restrictions so severe that these families constituted only 5 per cent of the roll (Piven and Cloward, 1971: 127). The family of an insecure worker could in fact fare better if the father 'deserted', allowing them to claim as a one parent family.

The variation of provision by state is argued by Piven and Cloward (1971) to have been established historically with a view to local labour needs. It is no accident, they argue, that the 24 states which allowed AFDC to unemployed men were located predominantly in the North, with four exceptions in the urban South. It is the rural South, however, which depends heavily on seasonal and poorly paid labour of black men and women. Low benefits in these states also served to keep black single mothers in the workforce, with the overall effect that in rural areas of the South blacks were under-represented on the AFDC rolls, and received generally lower benefits than whites (Piven and Cloward, 1971: 137). Piven and Cloward argue that there is a clear connection between local welfare practice and labour needs, reinforced by the principle of settlement which typically denied aid to those who had not lived in the state for at least one year.

They further argue that in the 1960s there was a system of 'bureaucratic deterrence' at work which intimidated applicants and led to withdrawal or failure to claim. 'For example, until the mid-1960s half of the applications for relief made in Philadelphia were rejected, and welfare rights lawyers estimated that half of the rejections had not been justified under existing statutes' (p. 156). The Moreland Commission on Welfare had found, in 1962, that claimants' relationship with officials was 'adversary' rather than 'helping' (cf. Howe, 1985 for the UK). Part of this problem is bound up with the surrender of commonly accepted rights of privacy by virtue of applying for aid, though eventually rulings were made against after-midnight raids to check for the presence of a man.

Major concern had arisen by the end of the 1960s over the unprecedented rise in AFDC rolls. 'During the 1950s the AFDC rolls rose by only 110,000 families, or 17 per cent. But from December 1960 to February 1969, some 800,000 families were added to the rolls, an increase of 107%' (Piven and Cloward, 1971: 183). Urban areas as a whole accounted for 70 per cent of the increase, but rural areas were not excluded, despite considerable outmigration. The rise was 175 per cent in northern urban areas, 121 per cent in southern ones, 87 per cent in northern rural areas, and 34 per cent in southern ones. Seventy-one per cent of this welfare increase in the 1960s took place in the four years after 1964 (Piven and Cloward, 1971: 185, 187). One assumption might be that the figures are explained by the migration from south to north; from regions of restrictive welfare practice to more generous ones, but such migration occurred predominantly in the 1950s, not at the time of the greatest expansion of rolls, nor were these migrants the typical claimants (Katz, 1989).

In one of the most contentious political statements ever D.P. Moynihan attributed the growth in welfare rolls to the breakdown of the Negro family, and a set of general circumstances he described as a 'tangle of pathology' (Moynihan, 1965). 'The steady expansion of this welfare program, as of public assistance programs in general, can be taken as a measure of the steady disintegration of the Negro family structure over the past generation in the United States' (quoted in Katz, 1989: 48). The figures, however, belie this account. Although black families were about 2.5 times more likely than white to be fatherless there had been no recent dramatic rise at the time of the report. There was a gradual increase from 19 per cent in 1949 to 24 per cent in 1959, and stability between then and 1964 (at 23 per cent) (Katz, 1989: 47). The increase in claims for AFDC could not principally be explained by the rise of eligible families, for in the late 1950s and early 1960s only a relatively small proportion of those eligible received such aid. Much of the rise was the result of the extension of aid to *previously eligible* families.

Lurie (1968) found that even if all new single mothers between 1959 and 1966 had received AFDC this would have accounted for only 10 per cent of the rise of cases over that period. Piven and Cloward (1971) instead see the rise as a political response to social disorder. Between 1950 and 1965 farm employment fell by 45 per cent, particularly affecting low-skilled black men and women in the South. There followed a massive migration to northern cities but over the main period of population movement the five urban counties which experienced the largest rise showed only slight increases in AFDC rolls. It was urban disorder and its electoral repercussions which brought the change and allowed on to the rolls the large numbers of eligible families previously excluded. Piven and Cloward argue that the rising population in northern cities and increased disorder, together with presssure from federal government, led to a loosening of restrictions on local relief. Welfare rights had emerged as a national issue which was taken up by the government as part of its Great Society programme.

THE WAR ON POVERTY

1964 to 1972 saw a large swell in anti-poverty programmes, and an increase in access to welfare relief. It is argued (e.g. Katz, 1989) that one of the motivations for this on the part of the federal government was the Democratic Party's attempt to win the newly available vote of previously disenfranchised blacks from the South. The movement of blacks from south to north meant the availability of new votes in the northern cities, whilst the spread of the franchise in the South increased the numbers of black voters there, from 11 per cent in 1962 to 17 per cent in 1969. A good deal of emphasis was placed on education and training, and the achievement of equal opportunity, but there was also an attempt to expand the availability of relief through federal intervention at state level. Improved information and awareness of rights was one fundamental change, and the 'storefront service centre' became prevalent.

General awareness of availability of AFDC rose, and there were three key Supreme Court decisions which affected claims (Katz, 1989: 107). The denial of welfare to mothers maintaining a sexual relationship was struck down in 1968; the one-year waiting period on arrival in a new state was ruled to 'penalise the fundamental constitutional right to state travel' in 1969; and in 1970 clients were ruled to be due a hearing before benefits could be stopped. The impact of these changes was reinforced by the Community Action Program dedicated to directing resources to the black ghettos; there was simultaneously a collapse of restrictions and an increase in awareness and information which together expanded relief rolls to an unprecedented extent. The proportion of applicants accepted for AFDC rose dramatically from 33 per cent in the early 1960s to 90 per cent in 1971 (Katz, 1989: 106). The spirit of this era is captured by the term 'Great Society'; 'maximum feasible participation' had been the goal of the Great Society anti-poverty programmes. That goal had almost been reached.

This argument did not, however, lay to rest the debate about the nature of the black American household, nor did increased access to welfare solve the poverty problem. In 1986 nearly one in three black Americans and one in four Hispanics lived below the poverty line (Katz, 1989: 126), and despite a fall in child poverty between 1960 and 1974 there has been a subsequent increase to 21 per cent in 1986. This Katz links this to the growth in single

parenthood. Such growth may not have been the major explanation of the welfare explosion of the 1960s, but developments since
then certainly show dramatic change. From 1970 to 1984 the
proportion of female-headed households rose nationally from 11
per cent to 16 per cent among all families, but the growth was
concentrated in the black population. For whites the increase was
from 10 per cent to 12 per cent, and for blacks from 28 per cent
to 43 per cent. This is not to say that poverty was entirely
concentrated in families of this structure or among the black
population, although both were disproportionately represented.
In 1986 69 per cent of the poor were white, as compared with
28 per cent who were black.

Since the late 1960s there has been a transformation in the
economic structure, reflected particularly in large cities; full time
employment in manufacturing dropped from 26 per cent in 1969
to 19 per cent in 1984. There was, however, considerable growth
in service sector work of all kinds. Part of the growth was in areas
of work requiring higher educational qualifications than the jobs
lost from manufacturing; service sector employment in finance,
insurance and real estate rose from 13 per cent to 28 per cent.
There was also a growth in lower level, poorly paid service sector
employment, largely in retail and hotel work, much of which was
taken by illegal immigrants. There was a new ethnic and spatial
dimension to the changing job structure; the superior employment
tended to be located in the suburbs and attracted a movement out
of the city centre by whites and better-educated blacks. There was,
however, some inward migration by lesser qualified blacks, to the
central areas of poor employment and lesser opportunity. Thus:
'Urban blacks experienced extraordinary rates of unemployment
or marginal employment, and to survive economically they called
in disproportionate numbers upon welfare programs, especially
AFDC' (Skocpol, 1988: 304). Yet fewer than half of the states
took up the option of including families with an unemployed man
among those eligible for AFDC, until 1990 when this provision
was finally available in all states.

The overall picture which emerged was a concentration of the poor
black population in the central city areas, with almost half of black
families headed by single mothers, many of whom were dependent
on AFDC. The assumption followed that it was welfare which
had caused this problem, encouraging idleness and illegitimacy,
and so AFDC became the focus of concern about an overtaxed

budget and a morally decadent (and mainly black) population. The concern is somewhat disproportionate to the costs, for expenditure on social security had grown very much faster, and from a higher base, than the costs of AFDC. In 1984 social security spending had reached a cost of $180.9 billion, as compared with $8.3 billion for AFDC. The attempts in the 1980s to curb public spending, however, had more impact on the latter than the former, and this reflects the familar distinction between the deserving and the undeserving poor. There was strong resistance to any erosion of social security though some small savings were made. AFDC fared worse, with reductions in both the amount paid and in the numbers judged eligible. The overall effect was a cut of expenditure of 12.7 per cent for AFDC, and of 6.9 per cent in unemployment insurance. Skocpol (1988: 296) states:

> Americans do not think of the federal government's public benefits adding up to an integrated system, applicable to all citizens. Instead, they sharply distinguish welfare programs from social security. And only social security has positive legitimacy as a state activity and comes close to being identified with full citizenship rights for Americans.

There is thus a polarisation in attitudes towards the major income support programmes of the United States, reflecting the perennial dilemmas of public assistance, which we have seen to be present throughout both the British and American history of social provision. Both countries show a growing reliance on means tested public assistance benefits, as opposed to contributory insurance benefits, and they share a common concern about the work incentive. There have been a number of initiatives intended to encourage AFDC recipients to remain active in the labour force, and Workfare, introduced in 1967, makes benefits conditional on work for many applicants. A similar arrangement is being actively considered in Britain. A major difference between the two countries, however, is that the overwhelming majority of public assistance homes in America are headed by single mothers. The other issue of public concern has therefore been the potentially disruptive effect of AFDC on marital stability, so as of 1990 all states offer AFDC to families with an unemployed father, though eligibility rules are tight. The basic welfare dilemma remains: does the provision of income for those in need encourage behaviour and circumstances which exacerbate the problems that policy seeks to address? This is a long-established concern for both British and American social policy, but has become the focus of a controversial debate about social justice and social inclusion in the States, which goes beyond the 'social citizenship' of Marshall's work.

LOSING GROUND

The writer who has most overtly taken up this issue in the US is Charles Murray (1984), whose book *Losing Ground* asks many of the questions commonly avoided by liberal academics and policy makers. For him the welfare dilemma is summed up in the following questions: 'How is a civilised society to take care of the deserving without encouraging people to become undeserving? How does it do good without engendering vice?' This approach is labelled the 'perversity' thesis by Hirschman, a common reaction to the Great Society programme: 'The exaggerated promises of that programme led to similarly exaggerated assertions of total failure' (Hirschman, 1991: 33). The argument is that poverty provisions had an effect directly in opposition to what had been intended. For Murray there are two major issues: the rising rate of never-married, black single parents, and the withdrawal of black youth from participation in the labour market. These combine in his concern that the rate of poverty was falling until the introduction of the War on Poverty, formally launched by Johnson in 1964. At this point the improvement ceased.

AFDC had been introduced under the New Deal as provision for widows, but its major increase throughout the 1950s and 1960s was among women who not only had never married, but who continued to reproduce (Murray, 1984: 18). Murray cites figures which show a sharp fall in the proportion of black two-parent families from 72 per cent in 1968 to 59 per cent in 1980. This he argues to be a factor of economic rather than racial difference, illustrated by the concentration of single mothers among families of the poor. His argument though seems to attribute the rise in the incidence of poverty to the rise in the incidence of this household structure. He argues that, historically, single parents have tended to experience high rates of poverty, then cites Green and Welniak (1982) who state: 'Changes in family composition have accounted for 2,017,000 additional poor families' (Murray, 1984: 133). There is a flaw in this argument if it is intended as an *explanation* of poverty. The true cause of poverty lies in whatever is the force behind the emergence of this particular household structure. The most likely explanation would seem to be the very high non-employment (and also mortality) rates of black youth – a distinctive feature of the current (1980s) generation of young blacks. While older blacks gained ground against vulnerability to unemployment, younger blacks (16–24) lost ground.

Murray attributes this pattern to the voluntary labour market withdrawal of black youth. Especially striking, he argues, is the fact that the major decline took place in the very tight labour market of the late 1960s. The fall in participation is not fully explained either by increased school enrolment nor by the discouraged worker effect. In making the latter point Murray argues that participation rates for blacks were stronger in the earlier and less prosperous period of the 1950s than in the buoyant economy of the late 1960s. Yet this fall-off happened at a time when other blacks were making advances in occupational status. Murray constructs his explanation for these patterns by way of a case study of the hypothetical couple Harold and Phyllis, before and after a number of welfare reforms which took place in the 1960s.

He reasons that before reform if a young woman became pregnant the options were either self-support through employment, self-support through AFDC, or marriage and dependence on a husband. Marriage or cohabitation disqualified the woman from claiming AFDC, and the best option for the couple was to stay together supported by the man's low-paid employment. By 1970 the income equivalent of AFDC had risen considerably, the claim was no longer jeopardised by the presence of a man in the house, provided he was not legally responsible for the child, and both woman and man were permitted some earnings without loss of relief. The rational conclusion, argues Murray, is for a couple to remain unmarried and to live off the woman's welfare claim. Furthermore, work incentives under AFDC, intended to encourage participation in the labour market, instead induce the working poor to take up welfare. A number of other factors are said to induce dependency.

'Status and money are two of the most influential rewards that society uses in order to manage behaviour' (p. 178). Murray argues, however, that the system of status in the United States shifted significantly in the course of the 1960s. Firstly, the boast of self-sufficiency, and particularly a man's ability to cater for wife and children, was undermined by explanations of poverty and unemployment which were based on social structural factors rather than on the characteristics and behaviour of individuals. This shift is argued to have eroded a major moral distinction: 'self-sufficiency was no longer taken to be an intrinsic obligation of healthy adults' (p. 180). Secondly, a related effect was the removal of the stigma which had previously attached to receipt of public assistance. There was no longer a requirement that the claimant be shown to be in some sense worthy of support. The alleged loss of this distinction is, for Murray, a bad thing; the poor have been homogenised. Finally, the extension of welfare programmes, notably food stamps, housing assistance, and Medicaid, turned all low-income persons into welfare recipients. Again this had the effect of blurring the boundary between the deserving and the undeserving, and removing the stigma of dependence – a distinction which he implicitly accepts can be sustained.

Murray sees this combination of factors as the debilitating aspect of black socialisation, fed by post-1964 social policy:

> Every assumption that a young black in the ghetto might make about his inability to compete with whites was nourished by a social policy telling him, through the way it treated him day to day, that he was an unresponsible victim. Society's actions were at odds with society's rhetoric telling him to be proud and to believe in himself. (1984: 187)

THE COUNTER-ARGUMENT

There are a number of opponents of Murray's position, and the general basis for a counter-argument has been summarised by Neckerman et al. (1988: 402) and Katz (1989: 153). Neckerman et al. point out that the introduction of AFDC predates the increase in black, female-headed families by about twenty years, but concede that liberalisation of regulations (e.g. the overruling of the 'man in the house' prohibition), together with increased benefits in the 1960s, could have stimulated out-of-wedlock child-bearing. They further argue, however, citing a wide range of empirical material, that there is no evidence at all to this effect (cf. Morris, 1990). Work by Ellwood and Bane (1985) suggests that high welfare benefits increase the chances of young single mothers living alone rather than with relatives, but cannot of itself account for the shift to single parenthood. Katz also challenges the assertion that welfare acts as an incentive to births out of marriage, for benefit rates fell steeply after 1972, and between 1972 and 1980 black children supported by AFDC fell by 5 per cent. Furthermore, births out of marriage rose for women not receiving welfare.

Murray's argument that welfare provision halted progress against the poverty rate is also challenged by Katz. Citing Jencks' (1985) reworking of the figures, he argues that Murray was wrong about the poverty rate; the 1950 rate was three times as high, and the 1965 rate twice as high, as the 1980 rate. Rising unemployment from 1968 onwards is argued to be the principal reason why the rate did not fall further. The related issue of changing employment structure is something which Murray neglects, and which is taken up by Neckerman *et al.* They note the severe mismatch between the jobs available and the skills of inner-city blacks (Kasarda, 1985; Fainstein *et al.*, 1992), and the severe decline in manufacturing and wholesale and retail jobs in central cities, especially in older northern cities. Employment in the suburbs expanded dramatically, as we noted earlier, and there was outmigration of middle-class residents and in-migration of rural southern blacks, ill equipped for such jobs as were available.

A wealth of research exists associating male unemployment with high rates of marital separation. The viability of marriage for inner city blacks is also undermined by a low ratio of men to women, high black male mortality rates, incarceration and substance abuse:

> Unlike white women, black women, and particularly younger black women, face a shrinking pool of economically stable or 'marriageable men'. These findings provide additional support for the hypothesis that the rise of black female-headed families is directly related to black male joblessness. (Neckerman *et al.* 1988: 408)

Murray would no doubt see this as support for his argument based upon the voluntary withdrawal of young blacks from labour force participation, and a shifting of responsibility away from the individual; blaming the system, as he puts it. His position is weakened, however, by the failure to address the role of changes in occupational structure and population movements in bringing about this situation.

He is finally criticised for being wrong in his calculations about the hypothetical couple, Harold and Phyllis. Katz argues that minimum-wage work throughout most of the country provided an income higher than welfare; twice as high in the South, and that Murray neglects to point out a 20 per cent fall in the value of the welfare package during the 1970s. Greenstein (1985) argues: 'in 1980 – even in Pennsylvania – Harold and Phyllis would have one-third more income if Harold worked than if he remained unemployed and Phyllis collected welfare.' Neckerman *et al.* also question the accuracy of Murray's calculation, notably the insufficient account taken of non-cash benefits such as food stamps available to the working poor, and his neglect of the deterioration in the relative advantage of welfare over work.

One puzzling point about the welfare system which is not directly addressed by Murray concerns the withdrawal of black youth from the labour market. The young unemployed are one group in American society who have no claim to state support as of right. The major welfare programme for the jobless is linked to the presence of dependent children, and has only recently been available in all states to families with an unemployed male. Whilst there are special programmes usually linked to training or work requirements, they are of limited duration and do not provide a reliable source of maintenance for those outside the labour force. In fact, withdrawal from the labour force would mean disqualification from such programmes. There is a sharp contrast with the British system of social support in which benefit has been available as of right to all the unemployed, regardless of family circumstances – though the conditions imposed on young people have increased of late. What then is the welfare incentive to remain out of employment in the American system, other than to father a child and live off AFDC claimed by the mother? Murray does not directly address this question, and AFDC seems unlikely to be a full explanation for the low labour force participation of black youth.

Quite apart from the criticism of detail, interpretation and explanation in Murray's work, an entirely separate issue of principle is at stake; how much should a government do in support of the needy? and where does the boundary between collective and individual responsibility lie? We discussed in the previous chapter the development of the idea of guaranteed social citizenship, which it was the duty of the state to provide for its citizens. The welfare state in Britain was, in its early stages, expected to achieve such an ideal, though there has recently been some retrenchment. This objective has never achieved the same degree of consensus in the States as in Britain, and welfare provisions have never been so fully developed. In America a different idea of citizenship and social inclusion which looks 'beyond entitlement' has begun to develop, raising the question of duties and obligations owed by citizens to their society.

THE OBLIGATIONS OF CITIZENSHIP

Mead's (1986) work, *Beyond Entitlement*, is a major example of concern with the obligations of citizenship. Like Marshall he sees the desirable aim of social policy to be the full integration of all citizens, and sees social separation as a worrying feature in the development of an underclass:

> Washington does give too much to the poor – in the sense of benefits given as entitlements. It also gives too little – in the sense of meaningful obligations to go along with the benefits. What undermines the economy is not so much the burden on the private sector as the message government programs have given that hard work in available jobs is no longer required of Americans. (1986: 3)

To function as full citizens people not only need to be guaranteed a reasonable standard of living, he argues; they themselves must achieve the capacity to learn, work, support their families and respect the rights of others. These obligations go beyond entitlement and distinguish the deserving from the undeserving poor. 'The idea of coupling benefit with enforcement of the common obligations might at last provide a political and ideological basis for a more effective social policy' (p. 14).

Mead's argument is that both the New Deal emergency measures and the design of social security legislation were based on the premise that the poor were fully competent to help themselves; that any other than temporary relief should be confined to the unemployable. The final barriers to self-help and opportunity were, he argues, removed by the efforts of the civil rights movement. His critical attention focuses on those members of the population who are long term welfare recipients; those with 'functioning problems': 'traceable to an unstable family life, marked by absent fathers, erratic parenting, and low self-esteem and aspiration' (p. 22).

The majority are black, but the explanation offered does not lie with ethnic identity. Like Murray, Mead highlights the withdrawal from the labour force by young blacks at the time of the Great Society programmes, leaving a hole which could only be filled by illegal immigrants (Mead, 1986: 37). He adopts the 'perversity thesis' to argue that 'through continued neglect of the functioning problem, social policy will begin to contradict itself. It will no longer serve democratic ends but may actually make the poor less free and equal rather than more' (p. 42). Poverty is attributed to family break-up, illegitimacy and the inability to get or hold jobs, not to structural circumstances. This does not address the points about black unemployment, mortality and incarceration raised by Neckerman *et al.*, except in so far as Mead asserts that the problem is behavioural and should be addressed accordingly.

Mead concedes that few men qualify directly for AFDC but can qualify for some benefits through training schemes, or job creation. Many of them, according to Murray, withdraw from such schemes, however, and Mead's argument about the creation of a mentality of welfare dependency seems on these grounds to be shaky. The solution, he argues, lies in work enforcement; the poor must not be seen as passive victims of their environment, background, etc. but must have positive requirements placed upon them which challenge their withdrawal from fulfilling the normal obligations owed to society. In 1967 and 1971 work requirements were placed upon AFDC recipients, but with work incentive schemes which made only partial deductions from benefit. In 1980 conditions were tightened, and Workfare required welfare recipients to work in compensation for the assistance they receive. Such procedures principally address the situation of single mothers, not young blacks, who receive little from the system in terms of income support as of right. It is the latter group which causes Mead most concern; they are argued to have withdrawn completely from the conventional expectations of society, in defence of a self-image which is stronger and more positive than could be supported in the low status, poorly paid jobs that are available to them.

Mead's view is summed up in one of his concluding paragraphs:

> The evils of slavery, racism and unregulated capitalism threatened the rights aspect of citizenship and prompted federal protections. The functioning problems characteristic of the ghetto – crime, non-work, family breakup – threaten fulfillment of obligations attached to the programs that support the poor. The

response should be federal obligations attached to the programs that support the poor. (p. 256)

For Mead, American society is entering into a fourth stage of citizenship (beyond Marshall's three), in which rights are sustained only by the fulfilment of obligations. There is still much potential for disagreement over where collective responsibility ends and individual responsibility begins.

Katz is critical of Mead for a number of reasons: the obligation of Mead's notion of citizenship soon becomes coercion, and poverty and destitution the means of compelling people to take dirty and low-paid jobs which they would not otherwise accept. Does a reasonable definition of full inclusion in society concede the right to dignified employment? For Mead unemployment is a subversive political act, poverty is equated with crime, indolence and immorality, and those who will not work must be made to work, or starve. This is a revival of the logic of the poorhouse and seems to offer no progress beyond the thinking of the nineteenth century. Mead does of course assume that anyone who wants a job can find one, though he also argues that the poorest jobs in American society are taken by illegal immigrants. Are these positions then considered to be too demeaning for workers with a claim to full membership of American society to accept, having embraced the standards of the whole? Mead paints a picture in which only 'outsiders', that is non-citizens already excluded from making a legitimate claim for an acceptable standard of living, will perform the menial services upon which such a standard of living for others depends. There is an implied contradiction here, expressed by Moon's argument: 'There is something deeply and undeniably unjust about a social order that necessarily frustrates fulfillment of the promises it makes' (Moon, 1988).

RIGHTS OR DUTIES

There are thus two competing ideologies and moral codes; one sees welfare as an unacceptable distortion of individual responsibility and therefore self-respect, and the other sees welfare as an unsatisfactory corrective to inequalities inherent in the social structure (cf. Moon, 1988). Moon sees the right to welfare and the achievement of self-respect as incompatible in American society, but leaves us with a problem rather than a solution: 'If we could organise the economy on some other basis – so that self-respect is no longer tied to work, or so that individuals could always find socially recognised and valued work, whatever their capacities or skills – then the central problem faced by the welfare state would disappear.' This would be to simultaneously overthrow the work ethic and the status system inherent in the achievement orientation with which it is associated.

Marshall raised the question of whether a capitalist system ordered by the rule of the market could be compatible with the guarantee of social rights, for it is largely the economic system which generates the inequalities necessitating the guarantee. Marshall's view was that social citizenship was in fact compatible with the free market system in that it could act as a corrective to inequalities. Material inequalities would not be eliminated, but the worst distress would be ameliorated: 'What matters is that there is a general enrichment of the concrete substance of civilised life. . . . Equality of status is more important than equality of income' (1950: 56).

The arguments considered above, however, all point to the role of individual responsibility, self-respect, the work ethic and the achievement orientation in the conception of social citizenship. Whilst a contributory system of social support can (with difficulty) be argued to protect the status which derives from self-sufficiency, a non-contributory system cannot. It becomes the mark of social exclusion, and is often seen in opposition to the values essential for an employment-based society.

Marshall argued that citizenship depended upon 'a direct sense of community membership based on loyalty to a civilisation which is a common possession' (p. 41). What Mead has hypothesised, however, is a society in which the disadvantaged, being denied the material benefits of inclusion, have withdrawn their loyalty and support for the values which condemn them as undeserving. Thus we return to the distinction which appeared at the outset of welfare development in both the US and in Britain: the distinction between the deserving and the undeserving poor, and the inevitable tension in any such provision bred of a conflict between the wish to provide and the need to maintain the incentive to work. In contrast to Britain, the US never fully embraced the idea of a guaranteed minimum standard of living as of right, was slow in introducing social insurance, and denied the right of support to unemployed men with insufficient contributions. A moral obligation to maintain women and children without support was, however, conceded, but as we have seen has been the source of much concern.

Fullinwider (1988) has identified two types of justification for welfare provision: non-instrumental reasons such as community, solidarity and social justice; and instrumental reasons such as social peace and human capital investment. The British welfare state is arguably closer to the former (though with elements of both) and the American system closer to the latter. A number of writers have pointed to the threats posed by the civil rights movement, and the concentration of unemployed black people in the northern cities, in emphasising the role of welfare as a means of containment. In the US we are now witnessing a critical review of such provision as exists, and the assertion that social harmony is not a one way process to be achieved by support for the needy, but requires from them some   positive assertion of their acceptance of the norms and values of the society in which they live. There are signs of this development in Britain too, with the erosion of support for the unemployed, and the tightening of eligibility rules.

Fullinwider wishes to argue in favour of plurality; i.e. in favour of a social order whose basic institutions allow all persons to realise their own ends:

> To the extent that individuals find that the larger system of institutions permits them to achieve their chosen ends and supports their causes, and that it is predicated on an uncon-ditional respect for their choices and causes, not on some overriding social goal that their choices just happen to further, they will come to value the system as good in itself. (1988: 278)

The question implicitly posed by the work of those such as Murray and Mead is whether the alleged choice of some to live outside of the norms and values of the majority is consistent with member-ship of the same society, or must they be coerced into conformity? For their critics the issue is whether full citizenship for all has really been achieved when some members of society face either the stigma of dependence or the indignity of unpleasant, low-paid and intrinsically unrewarding work in order to survive. Whether this state of affairs has produced a section of the population who stand – in terms of values, behaviour or life style – in some sense outside 'the collectivity' has been the foundation of debate about the underclass.

Chapter 4

The concept of the underclass

The two problems that drew Murray's attention – increased black lone motherhood, and the withdrawal of black youth from the labour market – have been at the centre of an explosion of American literature concerned with definitions and explanations of the emerging 'underclass'. The term itself suggests a group which is in some sense outside of mainstream society, but there is disagreement about the nature and source of their exclusion. One position (e.g. Murray) argues that welfare dependency has encouraged the break-up of the nuclear family household and socialisation into a counter-culture which devalues work and encourages dependency and/or criminality. The other position emphasises the failure of the economy to provide sufficient secure employment to meet demand, and the consequent destabilisation of the male breadwinner role. The former sees the source of exclusion as lying in the attitudes and behaviour of the underclass; the latter sees it as lying in the structured inequality which disadvantages particular groups in society. The precise nature of this structural disadvantage is itself hotly debated.

Public perceptions of this phenomenon recall the rhetoric of nineteenth-century England, and the two nations metaphor reappears with the argument that a second nation has emerged within black America: 'a nation outside the economic mainstream – a separate culture of havenots drifting further apart from the basic values of the haves'; 'urban knots that threaten to become enclaves of permanent poverty and vice' (US News and World Report, quoted in Katz, 1989: 197). Economic marginality, alternative values and deviant behaviour appear in some combination in almost all discussions of the underclass; deviance broadly embracing both criminal behaviour and single parenthood, which are implicitly associated. One of the problems facing attempts to unravel debate is the looseness of definition, which in turn complicates the problem of explanation.

The work of Ken Auletta has done much to popularise the concept of the underclass in the US, a term he applies to 'an estimated 9 million Americans who do not assimilate' (1982: xvi). By this he seems to mean those who cannot break out of poverty, and he identifies four (oft cited) groups:

1 the passive poor, usually long term welfare recipients (and presumably therefore lone mothers);
2 the hostile street criminals, drop-outs and drug addicts;
3 the hustlers, dependent on the underground economy but rarely involved in violent crime;
4 the traumatised drunks, drifters, homeless bag ladies and released mental patients.

Auletta embraces the notion of the 'underclass' because of its flexibility (p. 26), but this is the root of the conceptual problem: 'In the tradition of nineteenth century social critics who fused crime, poverty and ignorance into interchangeable eruptions of moral pathology, Auletta linked disparate groups into one class' (Katz, 1989: 201).

Auletta's emphasis is on their position as 'outsiders' in terms of both behaviour and material standard of living, but his definitions carry an implicit moral judgement. Each of his groups can potentially be condemned for their behaviour; the welfare dependent for their passivity, and the rest for their illegality, or lack of self-discipline. He rightly notes, however, that the core of debate revolves around whether the defining behaviour should be seen as the cause or the effect of their structural position (1982: 31). We saw in Murray's work an explanation which rested upon 'rational choice', with the ultimate responsibility placed upon the nature of welfare provision: 'It was wrong to impose rules that made it rational for adolescents to behave in ways that destroyed their futures' (1984: 219). The choice of dependency was further bolstered, he argues, by a socialisation which removes individual blame for failure, and this is what the post-1964 social policy is said to have done.

A cultural emphasis is much stronger in other earlier works which do not explicitly embrace the idea of an underclass. The most famous and frequently cited is probably Oscar Lewis's (1968b) explication of the culture of poverty. In his account the poor are characterised by a set of attitudes and behaviour which is initially bred of the experience of poverty, and represents an attempt to survive and come to terms with very limited prospects and resources. Once established, the behaviour, it is argued, develops into a self-perpetuating sub-culture which then plays a causal role in the disadvantage of the next population, 'By the time slum children are age six or seven they have usually absorbed the basic values and attitudes of their subculture and are not psychologically geared to take full advantage of changing conditions or increased opportunities which may occur in their lifetime' (Lewis, 1968b: 6). Similarly Banfield (1968), writing some years later, describes a lower-class culture which undermines both the ability to work and the stability of intimate relationships.

The 'culture of poverty' view is generally criticised for not placing the explanation of poverty where it really lies, in the economic structure, but instead encouraging a view of disadvantage as produced by a fatalistic orientation and lack of motivation on the part of the individual, so that poverty reproduces itself generation after generation. There are, however, elements of Lewis's position even in the work of those who seek to argue that the true source of inequality lies in the social and economic structure.

STRUCTURAL ACCOUNTS

The most prominent exposition of a structural explanation of the underclass comes from William Julius Wilson, though there are some contentious issues even within this general approach. The key disagreement here essentially revolves around whether the problems of the disadvantaged black population lie in their colour or their class position. Any argument which suggests that race is the ultimate source of disadvantage runs the risk of contributing to a revival of eugenics, as we see later in this chapter. Any argument which denies racial factors a central place, however, will also provoke opposition in seeming to deny the continuing effects of prejudice and discrimination.

In an early work, *The Declining Significance of Race*, Wilson (1978: 1) argues:

> Race relations in America have undergone fundamental changes in recent years, so much so that now the life chances of individual blacks have more to do with their economic class position than with their day-to-day encounters with whites.

In this book Wilson makes reference to 'a vast underclass of black proletarians – that massive population at the very bottom of the social class ladder plagued by poor education and low-paying, unstable jobs'. He thus conceptualises the 'underclass' as a black phenomenon, but to be defined in terms of vulnerability in the labour market, without reference to behavioural, moral or cultural factors. Though defined in terms of race, the underclass is explained in terms of class. The bone of contention in his argument is the assertion that the traditional barriers to black social mobility 'have crumbled under the weight of the political, social and economic changes of the civil rights era' (p. 1).

Despite this assertion Wilson does present data which demonstrate the severe employment disadvantage of many blacks in relation to whites. He argues that from 1954 the unemployment ratio for blacks and whites was roughly stable at two to one, and that in the mid-1970s black teenage unemployment was 2.5 times greater than that of whites. Furthermore, as unemployment rose the rate of withdrawal from the workforce by black teenagers also rose (pp. 91–2). The pattern is to be explained, he argues, by changes in the economic structure which affect lower-class blacks most by virtue of their occupational position, not their ethnic identity per se. A loss of central city manufacturing has been accompanied by a rise in white-collar employment, creating a demand for well educated workers but a decline in the need for the low-skilled.

At the time of disproportionately high black youth unemployment referred to by Wilson we also find an increased representation of blacks – from 16 per cent to 24 per cent from 1964 to 1974 – in high-level technical, professional and administrative positions (Wilson, 1978: 102), an example which is cited to emphasise class primacy in explanations of the 'underclass'. The expansion of opportunities for higher-grade black workers, however, had little significance at the other end of the class spectrum. In so far as opportunities in manufacturing have expanded, this has occurred outside the inner cities where poor blacks are concentrated, whilst there has been a 'flight to the suburbs' both by business and the more affluent population, black and white.

Wilson does address some of the behavioural and value related issues in asserting that poor blacks see work as a source of self-respect, but may be discouraged from job search by 'enduring lack of success'. He cites Liebow's 1967 study in support of this view, but concedes the further point that blacks may be disdainful of low-paying, menial work:

Workers today are less willing to accept the kinds of low paying and menial jobs that their grand-fathers or fathers readily accepted. To some extent this change in attitude is related to a revolution of rising expectations, not only for the black poor but for all citizens of America . . . many of the black poor have internalised the values emanating from the civil rights and black protest movements, values which promote black pride, and explicitly reject the view that disadvantaged minorities should be content with a system of unequal rewards. (Wilson, 1978: 108)

As others have also argued (e.g. Piven and Cloward, 1971), Wilson suggests that in this respect the expectations of southern blacks migrating to northern cities were lower than those of blacks born in the North, and it was this latter group which was more likely to resort to criminality or welfare as a substitute for unacceptable employment.

With regard to black single parenthood Wilson sees this too as a class-related factor not a black phenomenon per se:

The increase in female-headed households among poor blacks is a consequence of the fact that the poorly trained and educated black males have increasingly restricted opportunities for higher paying jobs and thus find it increasingly difficult to satisfy the expectations of being a male breadwinner. (p. 132)

He also cites Stack's (1974) claim that 'society's welfare system collaborates in weakening the position of the black male', though as we have noted, AFDC has, since 1990, been available in all states to households with an unemployed father present. Wilson, it would seem, does not dispute the behavioural characteristics which others (e.g. Auletta, Murray) have used in defining the underclass but sees them as secondary to the underlying structural forces of unemployment and poor prospects for inner city blacks. He further argues, however, that economic and political changes have so shaped the black class structure that it is increasingly difficult to speak of 'a single or universal black experience' (p. 144). This too is seen to have particular implications for the black underclass.

THE TRULY DISADVANTAGED

Wilson develops his argument further, directly addressing the culture versus structure debate on the urban underclass in *The Truly Disadvantaged* (1987). The definition offered in this later work differs only slightly from the one cited above:

> Individuals who lack training and skills and either experience long-term unemployment or are not members of the labour force, individuals who are engaged in street crime and other forms of aberrant behavior, and families that experience long term spells of poverty and/or welfare dependency. (Wilson, 1987: 8)

His emphasis has shifted from unstable employment to the absence of employment, and has expanded to include criminality and welfare dependence. Jencks (1992: 150) makes some interesting points about the importance of definition in estimating the size of the underclass: poor households headed by non-students aged under 65 who worked fewer than 48 weeks in the previous year totalled 5.7 per cent in 1968 and 8.7 per cent in 1987. Excluding the disabled reduces the percentages to 3.9 per cent and 6.7 per cent respectively, and including only those who had no work at all in the previous year brings them down to 1.9 per cent and 3.2 per cent. Wilson's later definition adopts the minimal approach which more or less corresponds to the four groups identified by Auletta. He asserts, however, that: 'Regardless of which term is used, one cannot deny that there is a heterogeneous grouping of inner-city families and individuals whose behavior contrasts sharply with that of mainstream America' (p. 7).

Whilst the conservative emphasis on an alternative value system, the adverse effects of government programmes and lack of individual initiative have certainly dominated debate, Wilson attributes this to the failure of liberal academics to fully engage in discussion. The tendency has been either to avoid the underclass issue entirely, to deny the validity of the term itself, to embrace selective evidence to deny the existence of an underclass, or to accept the existence of the phenomenon and to attribute it to racism.

Where liberal academics have most forcefully engaged in debate it has been to set up an opposition to culturally based explanations of the underclass phenomenon which identify a sub-culture of non-work, criminality and illegitimacy. The cultural approach is argued to be tautological in that values are inferred from behaviour, but the behaviour is in turn explained by the alleged sub-cultural value system (Wilson, 1987: 15). The opposing position is to emphasise the structural roots of the underclass experience, whether in terms of racism or class structure. Whilst Wilson accepts all of the features associated with the underclass in the conservative literature – high rates of lone motherhood, welfare dependency, poverty, unemployment and violent crime – he wishes to construct a more comprehensive and persuasive explanation than has so far been offered by either the left or the right.

Historic discrimination is argued to play a much stronger role than contemporary racism in such an explanation, one of its legacies being the presence of a large low-skilled black population in central cities. The migration of poor blacks from the South contributed to the concentration of a large black population at a time when immigration was being restricted. As a highly visible and expanding group for whom there was no clear occupational niche, the blacks became the object of stereotyping and resentment. The new arrivals from the South are said to have undercut the position of all blacks, and confirmed their position as a disadvantaged population at the lower end of the occupational scale, particularly vulnerable to structural changes in the economy. It is this legacy rather than active contemporary racist attitudes which Wilson sees to have laid the foundation for the emergence of a black urban underclass.

A population explosion among minority youth in city centres of the North happened at a time of economic restructuring and a shift in educational requirements for employment, creating a mismatch between those available for work and the types of opportunity in the labour market. In constructing this argument Wilson draws on the work of Kasarda (1986), and cites figures showing a concentration of unemployed teenagers in low income households, and a growing withdrawal of young blacks from the labour force (cf. Murray). At the same time there was an outmigration of non-poor blacks to the suburbs, setting up a concentration effect which created 'a social milieu significantly different from the environment that existed in these communitites several decades ago'

(p. 58). The non-working young blacks were thus deprived of contact with positive role models, and with the networks of association which could provide information, influence or encouragement in the search for work. The key theoretical concept here, argues Wilson, is not the culture of poverty but social isolation: 'the underclass exists mainly because of large scale and harmful changes in the labor market and its resulting spatial concentration as well as the isolation of such areas from the more affluent parts of the black community' (Wilson, 1991: 5).

It has been argued by some, however (Gans, 1990), that the term 'underclass' has become so hopelessly polluted that it should be dropped. Wilson (1991) takes up this position by substituting the term 'ghetto poor' and calling for 'a more concentrated focus on research and theoretical issues and less fixation on disputed concepts or labels' (p. 5). One aim of such research, he argues, should be to integrate structural and cultural approaches, though I would suggest that such an integration must inevitably give primacy to one or the other. In Wilson's account stratification in industrial society is not confined to material differences but also extends to differential cultural experience. This experience is 'accumulated from historical and existing economic and political arrangements', such that 'Group variation in lifestyles, norms and values is related to the variations in access to organisational channels of privilege and influence' (p. 1). Hence, there is a link between a structural position and a related cultural orientation and advantage. This is a powerful point to make, and implicitly contradicts any argument which suggests that a particular set of values and attitudes is causally prior to a position of structural disadvantage. However, Wilson's argument may integrate structure and culture but the explanatory force lies in the structure, and to this extent the structure/culture divide cannot be bridged.

His own research has now begun to emphasise the geography of the emergence of ghetto poverty, which has occurred mainly in two regions: the North-east and Midwest. Here the restructuring of industry resulted in the loss of blue-collar jobs, their only partial compensation by information processing, and a mismatch between central city residence and job locations. The net result has been a migration of the younger, better educated black population to the suburbs, and the emergence of a disadvantaged population, shed from manufacturing, trapped in the metropolitan centres. 'The central predicament of inner-city ghetto residents is joblessness reinforced by a growing social isolation in impoverished neighborhoods, as reflected, for example, in the rapidly decreasing access to job information network systems' (Wilson, 1991: 9). Jencks (1992: 123) also adopts the mismatch hypothesis and notes the difficulty inner city residents have in finding jobs which may be available in the suburbs, not easily accessible even should they succeed in their search. The situation is exacerbated by the failure of suburban manufacturers to advertise in inner cities, because they do not want the applicants this would bring them.

THE SIGNIFICANCE OF RACE

Jencks also draws attention to the fact that blacks are disadvantaged in relation to whites even when educational levels are the same. He suggests that part of the explanation lies in 'cultural conflict' (1992: 129), thus bringing race back to the centre of debate. Fainstein (1987) had some time earlier argued against the thrust of the underclass debate especially the work of Wilson (1987) and Kasarda (1985; 1986). The skills mismatch argument suggests that the black underclass is in part the product of a declining manufacturing base, a growth in 'knowledge based' industries from which the poorly educated are excluded, and the flight to the suburbs of an upwardly mobile black middle class. Fainstein wishes to stress the role of race in employment and career prospects by emphasising that whilst 'the black poor are sinking economically, the black middle class is not rising' (1987: 403). His argument is that urban blacks are not particularly dependent on a declining manufacturing sector, but suffer from segmentation into low-wage employment in whatever industry, and that this is a product of racial discrimination.

Fainstein's general argument is that the analysis of the position of poor blacks should not be separated from that of the more affluent. Thus he shows that black youth unemployment is not only disproportionately high for those from low income households, but is marked for those in households above the median income too (1987: 416). The income of blacks in the lowest quintile of income distribution declined in relation to whites, as did the second quintile, whilst from the mid-1970s onwards the position of the upper quintiles failed to improve. Fainstein's conclusion is that 'The evidence indicates that interracial differences outweigh inequalities among blacks, that the so called black middle class is very small when defined by income relative to whites, and that it has not improved its relative position in more than a decade' (p. 426).

He suggests that Wilson has exaggerated the bifurcation in the black population, for even in the best-paid occupational categories blacks are falling behind whites. Fainstein goes on to argue that the mismatch argument is inconsistent with the actual employment structure of the black population. Taking New York as an example he states that blacks are under-represented as compared with whites in the contracting manufacturing sector but over-represented in white-collar industries. He also attacks the suggestion that blacks worsen their own chances by their reluctance to move to areas of job growth in low level occupations, preferring to remain in areas paying higher welfare rates. Fainstein correctly points out that 'black males almost never receive welfare benefits, and they must be supported clandestinely on the meager allotments handed to females with dependent children' (p. 438).

He does cite the importance of networks both in providing job information, and in helping employers decide who to take on. As Wilson suggests, the neighbourhood concentrations of poor young blacks will act against them. But so too, according to Fainstein's argument, will racial prejudice inhibit advancement once in work, and any assertion that affirmative action has now achieved its aims fails to convince. Ellwood (1986) has advanced an argument somewhat similar to that of Fainstein in pointing out that differential residential proximity to jobs contributes little to explanations of black unemployment. Comparing unemployment rates of blacks in different areas of Chicago, Ellwood found the same rates of high unemployment, though Kasarda (1980) argues that the locations were not significantly different. However, as black and white unemployment rates in the *same* area of the city do differ Ellwood concludes it is 'race not space' which explains black disadvantage.

What we are seeing here is disagreement *within* a broadly structural approach to the underclass as to whether racial or economic factors provide the ultimate explanation. Whilst it seems undeniable that there have been structural changes in urban economies which have accentuated the labour market vulner-abilities of the poor black population, this account has seemed to some to ignore the continuing racial discrimination faced by the black population at all levels of employment. There does, however, seem to be general agreement that the black underclass is trapped in deteriorating areas of the city. Both the absence of a sufficient number of appropriate jobs and the flight of residents with better prospects have contributed to a neighbourhood deterioration which is likely to have the effects that Wilson predicts in his account of the social isolation of the underclass. In this sense a structural account based on either racial discrimination or economic restructuring meshes with a cultural perspectives which sees 'a commercially abandoned locality where pimps, drug pushers and unemployed street people have replaced working fathers as predominant socialising agents' (Kasarda, 1989: 45).

Wacquant and Wilson wish to emphasise that there are ghetto neighbourhoods which are distinctively different from black low-poverty areas. In the latter two-thirds are employed and one-third do not work, whilst in the former the proportions are reversed and as many as 61 per cent of adults are not employed (Wacquant and Wilson, 1989: 16). This is particularly interesting in the light of data on the incidence of long term joblessness. Jencks (1992: 155) reports that the rate of *short term* joblessness has been steady at about 7 per cent for white men and 10 per cent for black men during the 1963 to 1987 period, which suggests there are jobs available for some workers. Such a claim, however, seems to be contradicted by the steep rise in long term joblessness for black men in particular, from 1 per cent for white men and 4 per cent for black men in the early 1960s, to 2 per cent and 6–8 per cent respectively in 1985–7. For Wilson and Wacquant the explanation is not to be framed in individualised, moralistic terms concerning the lack of work incentive, but by 'cumulative structural entrapment', one dimension of which is the paucity of 'social capital'.

There is one other aspect of the interpretation of racial difference which should be noted here, and that is the incipient revival of a genetic approach. Jencks (1992) broaches this issue in *Rethinking Social Policy*, though his argument is unclear and misleading: 'The conclusion that blacks are five to ten times more likely than whites to commit most violent crimes is almost inescapable. This means that the genes determining skin colour are as closely correlated with criminal violence in the United States as genes determining gender' (p. 98). He fails to emphasise sufficiently the distinction between correlation and causality, and goes on to argue that: 'The examples of gender and race suggest that heredity and environment are not mutually exclusive explanations of human diversity, since genes can influence behaviour by influencing the environment' (p. 100).

The environment/heredity debate is familiar from our review of earlier treatments of the underclass and its equivalents, in which the genetic view ultimately failed to convince. Certainly where racial difference is concerned it would seem impossible ever to conclusively separate out any supposed genetic effect from the fact of visible social difference and all that follows in terms of stereotyping and discrimination. Lane (1985) for example, in a discussion of Philadelphia at the end of the nineteenth century, states that black crime rates were directly connected to exclusion from industrial and white-collar jobs, an account close to Wilson's argument for a link between economic and cultural explanations.

SINGLE PARENTHOOD

The other dimension of Wilson's position on the underclass is the challenge he poses to statements which associate changing family structures with a welfare effect. Wilson's position was touched upon in the previous chapter, but warrants further mention in the context of theoretical debate about the underclass. The argument currently advanced by writers like Murray (1984) differs from concern about 'female-headed families' in earlier work which emphasised the role played by structural conditions in undermining the economic prospects of the black population. Wilson's position is consistent with this view, highlighting male joblessness as 'the single most important factor underlying the rise in unwed mothers among poor black women' (1987: 73). The decreasing supply of what he calls 'marriageable men', rather than any welfare effect, is seen as the true explanation of expanding lone motherhood.

Economic conditions for black men have been deteriorating since the end of the Second World War, Wilson argues, and their labour force participation declined from 84 per cent in 1940 to 67 per cent in 1980. He cites evidence that the probability of divorce declines with age, largely because black joblessness, especially when combined with high mortality and incarceration rates, plays a very strong part in reducing the 'male marriageable pool index'. There has been a long term decline in the number of black men who are in a position to support a family. Wilson does, however, draw upon normative or 'cultural' explanations too, citing work by Hogan and Kitagawa (1985) which shows markedly higher rates of teenage pregnancy in 'high risk' social environments. The 'risk' factors are lower-class status, residence in poor inner city neighbourhoods, membership of female-headed homes, five or more siblings, a sister who is a teenage mother, and poor parental supervision of 'dating'. He also refers to data showing much later expectation of marriage among blacks than whites, which is linked to the 'poor marriage market' faced by black women (Hogan, 1983). Wilson interprets these findings as further evidence of the impact of social structural factors, although the emergence of normative expectations surrounding marriage and childbearing show a rather more complex dynamic; one which illustrates the association of structural and cultural forces as argued by Wilson himself (1991).

The argument advanced by Murray which places emphasis on the work disincentive of AFDC payments is weakened by the fall in value of this benefit since the early 1970s, and by its relative deterioration with reference to paid employment. Contrary to Murray's argument, states Wilson, real welfare levels did not rise throughout the 1960s up until the mid-1970s, remaining stable thereafter. By 1984 the combined welfare benefits were only 4 per cent above their 1960 level, and 22 per cent less than they had been in 1972. Meanwhile, since 1975, the Earned Income Tax Credit improved the work incentive for low-wage workers, who also benefited from benefits in-kind. So if the welfare/wage ratio did have an impact on household and marriage patterns then the trend to single motherhood should have reversed in the 1970s instead of increasing.

Jencks (1992: 158), however, argues that the weekly earnings of men in the bottom decile of the wage distribution fell by 25 per cent between 1970 and 1987, such that the wage/welfare ratio was little altered. He wishes to modify Wilson's account by suggesting that his argument about black joblessness makes the wrong comparison: 'Teenage boys have never earned enough to support a family, even when they had jobs, and they seldom married even in the 1950s . . . in 1960 less than 4 per cent of [16–19-year-old] black men who worked throughout the year were married.' He also argues that even according to Wilson's data the proportion of marriageable black men aged 25 to 44 remained stable in relation to women throughout the 1950s and 1960s at 70:100, and had fallen only to 63:100 by 1982; insufficient to account for the rise in single parenthood. According to Jencks it is the rest of the population that Wilson should be looking at, for between 1960 and 1980 the decline in the marriage rate among black men who worked regularly was almost as large as the decline among all black men. 'Marriage must therefore have been losing its charms for noneconomic reasons as well' (1992: 133). Furthermore, blacks constitute a declining proportion of welfare recipients, falling from 45 per cent in 1969 to 40 per cent in 1987 (p. 170).

Jencks's findings show an obvious defect in the underclass argument, and cast some doubt on the validity of an approach which revolves around concern with the decline of marriage, for marital instability is by no means confined to the lowest social stratum. This is not an issue upon which a clear dividing line can be drawn between the 'underclass' and the rest of the population. Nor necessarily is long term unemployment, if this is simply the result of vulnerability to particular aspects of economic change. This leaves only voluntary withdrawal from the labour force, and criminality, which may indeed reflect the rejection of a society which fails to live up to expectations. The polarisation of debate about the American underclass rests ultimately on a division between those who are concerned with the impact of economic restructuring and ethnic discrimination, and those who are concerned about the withdrawal and opposition of a particular group of the disadvantaged. One view examines the process of social and economic exclusion, the other considers the threat posed by non-participation.

THE BRITISH DEBATE

Though discussion about the nature and extent of underclass membership has been most fully developed in the US, the ideas that underpin it are by no means unfamiliar in Britain, not just in the upsurge of concern about dependency culture in the eighties, but through studies dating back to the 1960s and 1970s, and perhaps most notably the 'Cycles of Deprivation' work initiated by Sir Keith Joseph in 1972 as Secretary of State for Education. His concern was 'Why [it is] that, in spite of long periods of full employment and relative prosperity and the improvement in community services since the Second World War, deprivation and problems of maladjustment so conspicuously persist?' (Rutter and Madge, 1976: 3). This concern led to the hypothesising of the existence of cycles of deprivation. 'Perhaps there is at work here a process apparent in many situations but imperfectly understood, by which problems reproduce themselves from generation to generation . . .' (MacGregor, 1981: 93).

The empirical work undertaken to explore this phenomenon changed the terms of reference slightly, preferring disadvantage to deprivation, and problematising the question of whether deprivation was transmitted from one generation to the next in any directly observable way. It was recognised that disadvantage tended to be concentrated in inner cities, though the question of whether it was created there or attracted there was left open. The general orientation of the projects which developed centred on a set of interests very close to research into a 'culture of poverty' which is self-reproducing, and its contemporary equivalent, the idea of an underclass which recreates itself through poor socialisation and the absence of appropriate role models. For the 'cycles of deprivation' research a central question was: 'How far the continuing presence of disadvantage is due to some form of intergenerational continuity and how far it arises afresh in each succeeding generation' (Rutter and Madge, 1976: 303).

Whilst there was some evidence of familial continuity, this was slight, and more impressive were the concluding reservations expressed in the final report of the research, which are worth quoting at length:

> In the first place, even with forms of disadvantage where they [continuities] are strong, discontinuities are striking. At least half of the children born into a disadvantaged home do not repeat the pattern of disadvantage in the next generation. Over half of all forms of disadvantage arise anew each generation. On the one hand, even where continuity is strongest many individuals break out of the cycle and on the other many people become disadvantaged without having been reared by disadvantaged parents. (Rutter and Madge, 1976: 304)

It was also found that continuities are much weaker over three generations than over two. The research does not, however, dismiss the possibility of sub-cultural influences (p. 312), stating that these had some significance for delinquency and low IQ scores, but as a general explanation 'proved unsatisfactory'.

Similarly, genetic factors were found to be most applicable to IQ levels, but even there the impact of environment was strong. Genetic influences were negligible for scholastic attainment and minor delinquency. With regard to unemployment, the first emphasis was placed on the national and international situation, but with particular reference to regional variations. Job opportunities were therefore the major focus for concern, with personal factors bearing little significance for levels of unemployment. Beyond this, who suffers most may well be tied to individual features such as age, lack of skill, or physical incapacity, but may well also reflect the position and treatment of specific social groups, notably ethnic minorities. The report only touches upon the distinctive disadvantage of ethnic minority groups, but notes their concentration in poor employment and their consequently poor housing prospects, producing a tendency towards residential segregation (p. 314; cf. Wilson, 1991). This pattern features in other research from the 1960s (Rex and Moore, 1967), which showed housing discrimination against black and Asian workers, by estate agents, building societies and vendors, while the local authority points system systematically, if indirectly, placed them at a strong disadvantage. They were therefore forced to buy or rent in restricted areas, which led to both spatial and social segregation. The notion of an 'underclass' has for some time been used to refer to black people in this situation (e.g. Rex and Tomlinson, 1979: 16). It is further argued by Rex and Tomlinson that systematic disadvantage in both employment and housing lead to a neighbourhood activity which may be seen as an expression of a collective class awareness.

Rex and Tomlinson, in this way, set the debate in terms of class consciousness, and state that 'There is some tendency for the black community to operate as a separate class or an underclass in British society' (p. 33).

Their conclusion argues:

This underclass need not be seen as simply having negative qualities, namely those which follow from being left out of the native working class, but might be thought of as presenting . . . a wider political conflict, arising from the restructuring of a formerly imperial society. (p. 275)

This point has been taken up in more contemporary writing on, for example, the significance of new social movements based upon ethnic identity for the emergence of a political dynamic which supersedes social class (Gilroy, 1989). The statement by Rex and Tomlinson also places the underclass phenomenon in the context of the history and politics of labour migration, the definition and fear of outsiders, and the inferior position they necessarily occupy in the host society. There are strong resonances with some of the other conceptual themes identified in earlier chapters of this book.

THE BRITISH REVIVAL

Both the 'cycles of deprivation' research and the work on the black inner city underclass reach essentially structural explanations, the latter more strongly than the former. Rex and Moore are the precursors of Wilson's account of social and spatial segregation, whilst Rutter and Madge take up, but largely dismiss, a 'culture of poverty' account. As in America, Charles Murray (1990) has played a considerable role in placing the concept of the 'underclass' back on the agenda, but in a manner which bears little relation to the earlier work cited above. His contention is that 'The difference between the United States and Britain was that the United States reached the future first' (p. 2). With metaphors of 'plague' and 'disease' he argues that an underclass defined by illegitimacy, violent crime and drop-out from the labour force is growing, and will continue to do so because there is a generation of children being brought up to live in the same way. This, of course, is in direct contradiction to the findings of the 'cycles of deprivation' research, but an argument which reiterates Murray's analysis of the American underclass.

The first issue Murray addresses is that of illegitimacy, which he finds to correlate strongly with social class; areas with a high concentration of class V (unskilled manual) workers showed rates of about 40 per cent in contrast to 9 per cent in areas with a high concentration of class I household 'heads'. Unlike the situation in the US these births are not predominantly to black women, although blacks do have a somewhat higher illegitimacy rate of 48 per cent. But like the States, he argues, Britain has a high proportion of never-married women, as opposed to divorced women, who become long term benefit dependent. The interpretation of the statistics in terms of the availability of a father are not clear, in that 69 per cent of illegitimate births are registered by both parents. Benefit dependence, especially when combined with the absence of a father, is argued to provide poor socialisation into work identities.

The British benefit system has since its inception been more generous than the American system in that unemployed men, with or without children, can claim benefit as of right. Although young childless men are now required to undergo training it is not possible to make the direct connection between single parenthood and male unemployment that has been made in the US by writers like Wilson. It is the case, however, that single parents are granted a slightly higher benefit than two-parent families. Murray does point to the fact that benefits for single parents with one child under five at 1987 purchasing power rose from £22 in 1955 to £36 in 1987, and that during that time the social stigma attached to the status sharply declined. Changes in housing regulations in 1977 also gave single parents priority for housing under the 'homeless persons' category so that, overall, the difficulties of coping as a single mother have been much reduced.

Joan Brown is somewhat critical of Murray's position. Although agreeing with much of his data she points out that never-married mothers constitute only one-quarter of the total of single mothers, and that long term benefit dependence is greater for divorced mothers than for never-married mothers: 37 per cent of divorced mothers and only 27 per cent of never-married mothers had been on benefit for five years or more in 1987. Increased numbers of long term claimants among never-married mothers throughout the 1980s may, she argues, be linked to male unemployment, but to date never-married mothers do not spend long years on benefit because eventually they marry. For women aged 18–49 cohabitation rates have risen dramatically; 9 per cent of single women and 39 per cent of divorced and separated women cohabited in 1981, as compared with respectively 20 per cent and 52 per cent in 1988. 'Given these patterns, pointing the finger at single mothers – but not at divorced or separated wives – as an especial danger to society makes little sense' (Brown, 1990: 46).

Furthermore, the concentration of single mothers in certain areas she claims to be the result of housing policy rather than any 'contaminating' influence, such as Murray suggests. High priority cases for public housing tend to be offered the housing which is least in demand, the hard-to-let blocks or estates. This low popularity housing occurs in areas of generally poor appeal, hence the concentration of class V workers alongside high levels of single parents. Correlation does not always imply a direct explanatory link, and here it seems that housing policy is the mediating factor. As others have argued for the States, Brown suggests that marital, residential and child-rearing patterns are undergoing a revolution, which may pose a problem at the lower end of the income scale, but are nevertheless features of society as a whole.

Buck (1992) comes up with some interesting points about single parenthood by focusing on the interaction between household structure and labour market activity. Couple households generally showed higher employment and activity rates than other household structures, single person households had lower rates and single parents lower still. In 1986 42 per cent of lone mothers worked, in comparison with 50 per cent of married mothers, though single mothers were more likely to work full time than married mothers (Martin and Roberts, 1984). Changes in the distribution of household type would therefore suggest changing activity rates, if the rates for each household type remained the same. The rising inactivity rate between 1979 and 1986 shows a very different pattern from what might be inferred simply from household type, however. Though proportional increase was greatest for younger lone parents, the *rate* of increase was by far the greatest in couple households, especially those with younger children (350 per cent as compared with 40 per cent), while their share of all inactive households grew from 20 per cent to 38 per cent.

There are also data on the circumstances of young adults. In 1979 22 per cent of all households containing children over 16 showed at least one of these children to be employed, a proportion which rose to 23 per cent in 1986. For inactive couple households and lone parent households the proportions for 1979 were 26 per cent and 19 per cent respectively, falling to 21 per cent and 16 per cent in 1986. This might be seen as support for Murray's claim that the absence of a working male role model is damaging, though it may equally be the effect of social segregation such as that discussed by Wilson. As Brown has noted, single parents tend to be concentrated in undesirable housing. More significant is the fact that national rates of unemployment rose dramatically during the period considered, affecting all household structures.

Whilst the position of lone parents raises particular problems of social isolation and high rates of labour market inactivity, the most dramatic change was in couple households with an unemployed father. Households based on a married or cohabiting couple in 1986 still made up 71.7 per cent of working age households, with lone parents accounting for only 8.8 per cent and single persons 14.3 per cent. Particularly alarming to observers, however, are the concentrations revealed in the 1991 census (*Independent*, 10 April 1993) whereby in certain inner London boroughs single parent households contain one-third of all children, and rates of unemployment reach 25 per cent.

CRIMINALITY AND IDLENESS

'The habitual criminal is the classic member of the underclass. He lives off mainstream society without participating in it' (Murray, 1990: 13). Britain has a higher property crime rate than the US at 1,623 per 100,000 population in 1988 (i.e. directly affecting 1.6 per cent of the population) as compared with 1,309 for the States. Violent crime, however, is incomparably lower in Britain. This being said, Murray does little to actually integrate his statements about rising crime into his theory of the underclass. The purpose of quoting crime figures is simply to reinforce his argument that Britain is moving in the same direction as the US. The general point being made is that there is a group in society who fail to absorb, or who actively reject, the values and norms of the majority. Although his comments on the situation in Britain do not make an explicit link between crime, withdrawal from the labour force, and single parenthood, his concern about the last condition has largely been linked to fears of poor socialisation for the young.

Dahrendorf has also offered a definition of the underclass in which criminal activity is implicated:

> The underclass is the group which combines desolate living conditions and the lack of traditional bonds even of class with low skills and hopeless employment prospects. The result is cynicism towards the official values of a society bent on work and order. The underclass is not a revolutionary force, but one which will make its presence felt by crime, riots, and also by forming a volatile reserve army of militancy on either extreme of the political spectrum. (*The Times*, July 1985)

Elsewhere Dahrendorf says that there is a national social responsibility to ensure that young people have a stake in the future, notably through reasonable employment prospects. This he sees in Marshallian terms as a right of citizenship (1992: 58). Implicitly, then, crime rates are linked to a deteriorating economic climate, but the problem concerns the breakdown of social order. Dahrendorf's definition of the underclass involves some combination and association of the two.

Murray goes further: 'If illegitimate births are the leading indicator of an underclass and violent crime a proxy measure of its development, the definitive proof that an underclass has arrived is that large numbers of young, healthy, low-income males choose not to take jobs' (1990: 17). As with the nineteenth-century writings on the residuum a set of characteristics is loosely associated in such statements, but no necessary connection is demonstrated. The charge against the unemployed, and particularly the young unemployed, is that they have lost (or never developed) the will to work. This of course has been a fear which has always been evoked by provision for the jobless, though it has never been convincingly substantiated (a point addressed below). Murray's argument is that the distinction between the unemployed and the economically active is blurred by the fact that there are large numbers of unemployed people claiming benefit when no job would tempt them to work. Others really are working, in the 'black economy', and so do not count as truly unemployed.

Murray also makes the far from original discovery that unemployment and social class are associated. He uses the term 'economic inactivity', though his comments (noted above) suggest that he is interpreting this broadly, to include unemployment. Either way there are a number of possible reasons for his findings. Using census data from 1981 for municipal districts he asserts: 'You will find many more working-age people who are neither working nor looking for work in the slums than in the suburbs' (1990: 18). If he is referring to the officially defined economically inactive, then this category is made up principally of the elderly retired, early retired, long term sick, and the disabled. The reason why these groupings are likely to be higher for unskilled manual labourers (social class V) is that their experience in paid work is responsible for early deterioration in their health and withdrawal from the labour force.

If Murray is defining inactivity to include official unemployment, then it must be noted that there has long been an association between social class and unemployment: the lower down the class hierarchy a worker is the more vulnerable he/she will be to unemployment. For 1986, Britain's peak unemployment year, skilled manual workers made up 38 per cent of the economically active male population, but 41 per cent of the male unemployed. Semi-skilled workers accounted for 13 per cent of economically active males and 27 per cent of the male unemployed, and unskilled workers accounted for 3 per cent of economically active men and 11 per cent of the male unemployed (Morris, 1991). For women the highest concentrations were similar but more marked among the semi-skilled, who constituted 22 per cent of the economically active female population and 36 per cent of the female unemployed. The less job-specific skill a worker has, the more easily he/she will be replaced, so when redundancies are called for the class V worker will be the first to go. With redundancy pay linked to wages and length of service these workers will also be the most cheaply disposed of. Accentuating this source of vulnerability is the fact that trade union protection is more likely among skilled workers than unskilled workers, with professional workers even better protected. The reasons are not unrelated to the first point about expendability. There is a regional, municipal and even ward-level pattern to this because of the role played by large manufacturing conurbations in Britain's economic history, and because of an interaction of the labour market with the housing market.

The highest concentration of unemployment throughout the 1980s has been in areas most affected by the decline in heavy manufacturing industry; areas in which employment for male manual labour (both skilled and unskilled) has been predominant. In so far as new employment has been attracted to these areas it has been in service industries, with a high concentration of part time work, which has anyway been nowhere near sufficient to offset the job loss from manufacturing. Part time employment is usually taken by the wives of employed men in households where one income is insufficient, rather than by the wives of unemployed men (Irwin and Morris, 1993). The minimal housing choice of the low income unskilled workers, not to mention the unemployed, leads to their concentration in particular parts of town and even on particular housing estates, thus contributing to the clustering of the workless population alongside other vulnerable groups, notably single parents. One implication of the spatial concentration of unemployment is that the unemployed are increasingly likely to have contact largely with other unemployed people, and this negatively affects prospects for mutual aid and for access to new employment (Morris, 1992).

DEPENDENCY OR FRAUD?

As in Murray's account above, one view of the unemployed underclass is that many of them claim benefit despite the fact that they have no intention of seeking or accepting employment. Another view merges the unemployed with the criminal category of the underclass, by asserting that they are in fact working and claiming benefit illegally. Both these views have also been expressed by the Department of Employment:

> There is evidence that a significant minority of benefit claimants are not actively looking for work. Some are claiming benefit while working at least part-time in the black economy. Others seem to have grown accustomed to living on benefit and have largely given up looking for work, despite the high level of job vacancies which are increasingly available throughout the country. (1988: 55)

Fears and allegations of this kind grow as unemployment rises, and so charges that over-generous welfare has created a 'dependency culture' in Britain, consisting of people who have lost the will or capacity to work, sit alongside charges that many of the unemployed have been working all along. Implicit here is the idea that there is at least a section of the unemployed, in Murray's account an underclass, which subscribes to an alternative set of values based on either dependency or fraud.

One suspicion surrounding unemployed claimants is that since they are working they have two incomes: one earned and one unearned. The extent of abuse of this kind has been the subject of somewhat inconclusive speculation, complicated by the fact that activity in the 'informal sector of the economy', i.e. activity that bypasses national systems of accounting, are by no means confined to the practices of the unemployed (see Cooke, 1989). If there is an alternative culture in operation, based on fraudulent practices, it goes far beyond benefit claimants. There was optimistic speculation in the late 1970s and early 1980s (Gershuny, 1979; Pahl, 1980) about the capacity for areas of work outside formal employment to replace work lost in the formal sector. Later research on this issue (Pahl, 1984) argued that the distribution of opportunities in the informal sector of the economy was biased away from the unemployed, and dependent on skills, contacts and resources more commonly found among those with formal employment. Speculation continues; in 1981 the Rayner Report estimated that 8 per cent of unemployed claimants were unlawfully working and claiming benefit, and in 1989 Norman Fowler estimated up to 10 per cent (*Guardian*, 2 August 1989).

Ethnographic data on unemployment indicate that some unemployed claimants take occasional opportunities for paid work, though the extent to which this occurs is by no means clearly established. Jordan *et al.* (1992) emphasise the enduring significance of work for the unemployed: 'The men described themselves as active, needing to work to fulfil their personal needs as well as their roles as providers for their households. Idleness is characterised as boring and destructive of identity and self-respect' (p. 99). However, 'This need to remain active, alongside the requirement to provide an adequate income for the household, is used to legitimate work for cash while claiming benefit on grounds of unemployment' (p. 101). It should be noted that Jordan's sample contained only 11 unemployed men, and the details he gives are rather sketchy. McLaughlin *et al.* (1989: 82) found that only eight out of 110 individuals had at some stage had undeclared earnings, whilst a further three had peformed work for payment in kind. Morris (1984: 507) found that over a period of 18 months 12 out of 26 unemployed men had had some opportunity for informal earnings, though not for regular work, and often only 'odd jobs' for friends. This was in a sample of relatively young married men, for whom the pressure to augment income, and the opportunity to do so, is likely to be greater than in other sections of the population. Jane Ritchie (1989) found only one instance of regular informal earnings out of 30 cases of unemployment, but there was some incidence of occasional work or odd-jobbing. The willingness to accept such opportunities increased with extension of unemployment and financial hardship. All of the studies referred to stress that the work was usually of relatively short duration, often not more than a day at a time, a finding also noted in research in the north-east of England (Morris, 1987). 'Earnings tended to be occasional lump sums rather than regular weekly incomes and as a result although individuals have earned more than the legal amount in one particular week, over a longer period their earnings have often averaged out at less than this amount' (McLaughlin *et al.*, 1989: 82).

Evidence of this kind points to an enduring need for the self-respect attached to work, and to the contradictions of a benefit system that wishes to preserve independence but stifles initiative in an economic climate in which regular employment for a certain section of the population is simply not a feasible aim. There is also increasing evidence in the UK of the unemployed resorting to loans at extortionate rates of interest in their desperation to survive on benefit (*Independent*, 15 December 1992). Much of the paid work available to unemployed men is casual employment for a matter of a few days only, or at most weeks, so the attraction of not declaring earnings is quite clear:

> What would appear to be the obvious (legal) alternative – that is, signing off when starting a short spell of work, and signing on again when it is over – is perceived as both risky and disruptive for the limited amount of income that such work would bring. Considerable time and anxiety has to be invested in 'un-claiming' some benefits, claiming new ones, then reclaiming old ones. And of course delays in the processing of claims may mean periods when the households have neither earnings nor benefits. (McLaughlin *et al.*, 1989: 83)

THE INCENTIVE TO WORK

As noted above, alongside definitions of an underclass based on fraud are fears that a dependent underclass exists in which potential workers prefer benefits to employment. A softer version of this argument is the notion that workers are pricing themselves out of jobs and have an unrealistically high 'reservation wage', i.e. the lowest wage at which they would accept employment. The question of conditions of employment and levels of pay was touched upon in an earlier chapter in connection with the issue of the rights and obligations of citizenship. Does an obligation to work extend to any work, whatever the terms and conditions, or is one of the rights of citizenship the right to command a reasonable wage – one sufficient to secure a reasonable standard of living – and in that sense to facilitate inclusion in the social and cultural expectations of the community of membership? The argument about workers pricing themselves out of jobs is anyway too narrowly economistic, for a number of studies illustrate the significance placed on employment for a sense of personal worth and of pride in earning a living, which suggests that the wage is only one of many reasons for working (e.g. Morris, 1985; Deacon and Bradshaw, 1983; Jordan *et al.*, 1992).

Micklewright (1986) has reviewed evidence from a number of studies attempting to test the reservation wage/benefit relation and concludes:

> The evidence from microdata studies published in the 1980s has clearly been conflicting and no safe conclusion could be made at the present time about what the effect of benefit really is. . . . The general message . . . is that during the 1970s variations in people's benefit payments (or in the relation of these to wages) were not associated with large differences in their duration of unemployment. (p. 69)

He goes on to argue that 'The fact that cuts in benefit have occurred in the 1980s but have led to no falls in the level of unemployment is only considered by some as being evidence that far more severe measures are required.' As with the American data on AFDC, the behaviour of claimants did not follow the path that an economistic account of behaviour would predict; the value of benefits fell without a corresponding fall in the number of claimants.

There is research which has reported a concern that potential wages should be in excess of benefits, with claimants taking little account of the benefits available in the British system to the working population (J. Ritchie, 1989). This latter point is itself of interest, since generally speaking people wish to avoid claiming benefit. This is particularly true where the potential claimant has had recent experience of unemployment; there is a wish for independence. (Davies and Ritchie, 1988: 6). The validity of the reservation wage argument is challenged by data from a number of other studies. McLaughlin *et al.* (1989) for example, found mixed responses among unemployed men: 'Half of the men gave reservation wage levels which were above the level of their current [benefit] income and half which which were below' (p. 98). Although expectations were low in relation to average earnings they were high in relation to the jobs on offer. Nevertheless, of the 30 relevant men 19 had applied for jobs with wages lower than their stated reservation wage, and five for jobs offering wages at that level. An earlier DHSS cohort study of the unemployed had concluded that 'Self-reported reservation wages appear to be a poor guide to behaviour in the face of actual job offers. Judged by their behaviour a significant proportion of unemployed men have a very volatile view of acceptable wages' (Moylan *et al.*, 1984: 113). Marsh's (1990) study of the Chesterfield labour market found that most of the jobs on offer fell below the Council of Europe's decency threshold, and many offered pay lower than recruits would receive on benefit. Respondents nevertheless expressed high levels of satisfaction with their work. Heath's (1992) study of attitudes among the underclass found no evidence of a culture of dependency, and low standards with regard to acceptable jobs.

One view of the issue of reservation wages and low pay is that if benefits fall low enough then the unemployed will start to accept jobs they would not previously have considered, and it will become financially feasible for employers to create work which at higher wage levels would not have been possible. However, despite falls in the value of benefits over the last decade for many claimants, unemployment has remained high and is currently rising again, after a dip in the late 1980s from the 1986 peak. Seventeen recent changes in unemployment provision have been detrimental to the unemployed (Atkinson and Micklewright, 1988), while the linking of benefit rates to prices rather than wages has meant that claimants do not share in the generally increased standards of living available to the majority of workers through wage rises above the rate of inflation. This has led to a polarisation in society such that the majority employed population grow more affluent, while unskilled workers and the unemployed have not been able to share in this improved standard of living.

Field (1989) has appropriated the notion of the underclass to make this point; the underclass is not principally to be defined as a problem of social order, or as a group embracing an alternative value system. It consists of those who have been excluded from the increased affluence of the majority population:

> They increasingly live under what is a subtle form of political, social and economic apartheid. Indeed, the emergence of an underclass marks a watershed in Britain's class politics. Today the very poorest are separated, not only from other groups on low income, but, more importantly, from the working class. (1989: 4)

This is one attempt to integrate the notion of the underclass into a broader conception of class-based social stratification.

STRATIFICATION THEORY AND THE UNDERCLASS

Unemployment has always posed a problem for classificatory schema based on occupational ranking, and the notion of an underclass has been adopted by some in an attempt to deal with this problem. An influential article by Runciman (1990) argues that below the two working classes (i.e. the skilled and unskilled manual workers) there is a quite distinct 'underclass'. This term, he argues:

> stand[s] not for a group or category of workers systematically disadvantaged within the labour market but for those members of British society whose roles place them more or less permanently at the economic level where benefits are paid by the state to those unable to participate in the labour market at all. . . . They are typically the long-term unemployed. (p. 388)

I have criticised this position elsewhere (Morris and Irwin, 1992), for strictly speaking Runciman's definition applies not to the unemployed, who are at least notionally still participant in the labour market, if unsuccessfully, but rather to those more conclusively outside: the aged, the long term sick, and the severely disabled.

Smith (1992) adopts an approach similar to that of Runciman. He rejects a culturally based *definition* of the 'underclass', to argue that 'At a minimum, the idea of an underclass is a counterpart to the idea of social classes, and acquires its meaning within that same framework of analysis.' But 'The underclass are those who fall outside this class schema, because they belong to family units having no stable relationship at all with the "mode of production"' (p. 4). The question of whether cultural difference attaches to particular class positions he argues to be a matter for empirical enquiry, asserting however that 'empirical studies do show that the cultural differences between social classes are large and all embracing' (p. 5). Cultural distinctiveness and stability of membership he sees as an essential part of social class.

Gallie (1988) also takes up the issue of a cultural cohesiveness or collective self-awareness as a defining criterion for the existence of an 'underclass'. His starting point is a definition offered by

Giddens (1973), and explicitly rejected by Runciman: 'The "under-class" is composed of people who are concentrated among the lowest-paid occupations, or are chronically unemployed or semi-employed, as a result of a "disqualifying" market capacity of a primarily cultural kind' (Gallie, 1988: 465). He addresses the question of whether the 'flexible' (i.e. non-standard) employment patterns and long term unemployment which have characterised the 1980s offer a sufficient basis for the formation of a distinctive 'underclass' in the sense captured by Giddens. His conclusion is that the structural position exists but the cultural underpinnings do not. The populations most affected by insecure and/or non-standard employment are ethnic minorities, women, and the unskilled, white male working class. But for different reasons, largely concerning internal fragmentation or lack of cohesion, he suggests, none has the potential to develop a distinctive culture or consciousness.

In conclusion Gallie argues that predictions about the future formation of an underclass were based upon an aggregation of different types of labour market experience for contrasting groups, leading to an underestimate of the internal heterogeneity and likely diversity of interests. Collective self-awareness of either the unemployed or those particularly disadvantaged in employment is unlikely to emerge. Here Gallie touches on a problem Gans (1990: 274) has also remarked upon: 'underclass is a quite distinctive synthesising term that lumps together a variety of highly diverse people'. In Britain debate has been more sharply divided between concerns about the rather technical issues of classificatory schema and class formation, and the political and rhetorical concerns with social order and the threat posed by an (allegedly) emergent 'underclass'. Disagreements about definition may be close to the evasion tactics of some 1970s liberalism, which Wilson condemned. But a key underlying question which emerges does help to advance debate: where (if at all) can a dividing line be drawn between standard social class positions and the excluded 'underclass'?

One question of definition is raised by a view of the 'underclass' which includes the underemployed and insecurely employed together with the long term unemployed. My own research in Hartlepool (Morris and Irwin, 1992) shows that although there is a distinctive section of the population suffering from frequent and involuntary job change they differ significantly from the long term unemployed. A far higher proportion of the insecurely employed are skilled workers, and their periods out of work are generally temporary. They experience unemployment but are more successful in the search for work than the long term unemployed group, although that work often turns out to be unreliable. The social class profile of this group is similar to that of the secure manual workers; both groups are made up predominantly of skilled workers, but the fragmented nature of their employment history shows that they are much more vulnerable to job loss.

The insecure workers might be argued to constitute an underclass in Gallie's rather than Runciman's terms, by virtue of chronic insecurity and repeated unemployment. For this reason they stand apart from the secure workers, although their social class position as defined by skill would place the two groups together. As compared with the long term unemployed, however, they are clearly advantaged both by their possession of skilled status and their facility for finding work. The two groups could not therefore be placed together in a generalised category of the 'underclass'. Nor does this seem an appropriate term for the long term unemployed, whose position is explained by local economic decline, their vulnerability by virtue of lack of skill, and their paucity of work-based informal contacts.

Conventionally, unemployment has been dealt with in class schema by according the unemployed worker a position with reference to his (or her) normal line of work or most recent job. Those who have never had employment, and who lack job-specific training, pose a real problem here, though this is not the case for the majority of the long term unemployed. We noted earlier the well established correlation between lack of skill and the experience of unemployment. As I have suggested, the probable reason for this concentration of unemployment among the unskilled is the fact that the unkilled workers are most vulnerable to job loss being, from the point of view of the employer, the most easily replaced. As low-paid workers they also make for the cheapest redundancies. To separate them from their conventional class position as unskilled workers and designate them an 'underclass' is not helpful in attempts to explain their experience in the labour market, or its underlying dynamic.

Placed in the context of the above debate the use to which the term underclass has been put often appears to have been misplaced. The issues commonly addressed in relation to the underclass have principally been concerned with social order and the maintenance of the dominant value system, and not, strictly speaking, with social class. One question revolves around how far those most disadvantaged in material terms actively opt out of the norms and values endorsed by society as a whole. The counterpart to this is at what extreme of disadvantage does it become unreasonable to expect such normative participation? A separate question is how those excluded from standard, secure employment can be integrated into established conceptualisations of social class.

Chapter 5

Gender and the underclass

Gender related issues are ever present in conceptualisations of the underclass, and though rarely directly addressed the differential treatment of men and women in debate usually connects in some way with established views of socially appropriate roles and behaviour. This ultimately results in an unresolved ambiguity concerning society's expectations of its citizens. Malthus, for example, placed a lesser responsibility on women in his moral condemnation of the 'redundant population', seeing them as the 'more virtuous half of society', and as men's uncomplaining supporters. In other work, however, women appear – usually as prostitutes – among the social outcasts of a 'residuum', defined largely in terms of moral failure, as for example in Mayhew's category of 'those that will not work'. For Mayhew 'prostitution is the putting of anything to a vile use . . . the base perversion of a woman's charms, the surrendering of her virtue to criminal indulgence' (quoted in Himmelfarb, 1984: 341). He was writing at a time when the developing gender ideology placed upon women a responsibility for the moral education of the next generation. In this schema the 'essential nature' of women was strongly associated with a domestic and socialising role: 'The moral influence of woman upon man's character and domestic happiness [was] mainly attributable to her natural and instinctive habits' (Peter Gaskell, 1833, quoted in Poovey, 1989: 7). By the end of the nineteenth century even the poverty studies placed strong emphasis on the mother's role both as moral educator and as budget manager, each role offering a potential solution to poverty.

Ideas of this kind may be expressed less strongly in contemporary literature but they have by no means disappeared completely. Certainly we have seen in the work of Charles Murray a view of the underclass rooted in the alleged failure of the single mother household in the task of socialisation. Gilder (1986: 169) states quite explicitly that 'woman's morality is the ultimate basis of all morality', and even that 'The woman's place is the home, and she does best when she can get the man there too, inducing him to submit most human activity to the domestic values of civilization.' In contrast, Novak's (1987: 16) emphasis is on the family, and he argues that 'a failure to learn habits of self-mastery, work and citizenship at home leads to the habit of non-work, hustling or crime. The family is the matrix within which the citizen is well-formed or misshapen.' The single mother is implicated in the failure to instil a work ethic, and held responsible for the reproduction of a generation of young people who subscribe to an alternative set of values, rejecting the standards and norms of their own society. This account is part of a gendered view of disadvantage cast in terms of what Harrington (1984) describes as 'violent men and immoral women'.

It is commonly held that single parenthood is one manifestation of what Roche (1992) terms the 'deregulation of sexuality' (by which I take him to mean the deregulation of reproduction), though this is a contested position, as we shall see later. Divorce, illegitimacy and teenage pregnancy are argued to be part of this pattern, and Roche (1992: 100) notes that 'The rates for these indicators of "family structure breakdown" tend to be far higher among the American underclass than among the general population.' This statement is confusing, however, in the context of a literature which *defines* the underclass by reference to household structure, which is in turn used to explain poverty; the mistake of treating a correlation as a cause. Harrington challenges the stereotype that 'welfare mothers are promiscuous and immoral women who have huge families in order to get more money from welfare' (1984: 201) and offers an alternative gendered reading. He notes analyses which see divorce, separation and childbearing out of wedlock as major causes of welfare dependence, but argues: 'In almost all of these cases, women are left with unsupported children and, contrary to the myth, it is not their decision, but the man's, that pushes them under the poverty line' (p. 194).

Much of the US debate revolves around the role of welfare in this complex of influences: whether it subsidises and encourages 'immoral' behaviour, or whether it is an inadequate last resort for single mothers: 'Ironically, whereas AFDC was originally designed to allow single mothers to replicate the [traditional] behaviour of married women – that is, to stay home with their children – it currently functions to separate the two groups further' (McLanahan and Garfinkel, 1989: 101).

The socialisation issue has been tested out by research which examines the role of mother-only families in the growth and perpetuation of an urban 'underclass', consisting of those who 'operate outside the mainstream of commonly accepted values' (Auletta, quoted in McLanahan and Garfinkel, 1989). The findings are not entirely conclusive. Research in the 1970s found welfare dependency to be relatively short term; whilst almost 25 per cent of the population spent at least one year in poverty, only 3 per cent were poor for at least eight out of ten years. This suggests that the poor population is changeable in composition, which weakens any likelihood of a self-generating sub-culture, but the argument was challenged by Ellwood and Bane (discussed in McLanahan and Garfinkel, 1989).

In their review of the evidence Ellwood and Bane find that in 1987 one-third of single mothers could be classified as weakly attached to the labour force, of whom 56 per cent will be dependent on welfare for ten years or more, yielding 18 per cent of current single mothers. They then calculate that about 60 per cent of the daughters of this 18 per cent will themselves receive welfare for at least one year, 24 per cent for ten years or more. These leaves us with 4 per cent of the daughters of current single mothers who are likely to fall into long term welfare dependency in the next generation. Ellwood and Bane do, however, report a growing residential concentration of single mothers, with poor access to community and educational resources, and some evidence that children from mother-only families show greater acceptance of single parent status than do other children. They do not dismiss the possibility of distinctive cultural attitudes, but implicitly question an explanation rooted in the socialisation role of the mother.

THE FEMINISATION OF POVERTY

A growing literature on the feminisation of poverty in the US places a very different interpretation on the concentration of poverty in lone mother households, and the designation of this group as part of a growing underclass. The factual data on the distribution of poverty by household type is uncontested, and has been summarised up to 1984 by Rodgers (1986). Between 1959 and 1984 the number of female-headed families with children increased by 168 per cent, while male-headed families increased by only 7 per cent. By 1984 one in five families with children under 18 was headed by a woman; 16 per cent of white families, 25 per cent of Spanish origin families, and 52 per cent of black families. More than half of all the poor children in America live in female-headed families, as compared with 25 per cent in the late 1950s and early 1960s. There is a distinction by ethnic identity, with 68 per cent of the black poor in female-headed families as compared with just over 40 per cent for white and slightly more for Spanish origin families.

One obvious question is whether the rise in female-headed poverty is a manifestation of a shifting of poverty from other household structures, and here there are differences according to ethnic origin. In the white population the poverty rate for male-headed two parent families has been stable (to 1984) at about 8 per cent, and rose slightly for sole father families to 10 per cent. The rate for female-headed families has also been fairly stable at about 25 per cent but the rising base has meant an increase in the numbers affected (0.7 million, or 52 per cent). Here the feminisation of poverty is the result of a growth in this household type, with roughly stable poverty rates across the population. The picture for the black population is different, showing a more marked polarisation, with poverty rates among two parent families falling (from 33 per cent to 13.8 per cent between 1966 and 1984), and rising for sole mother families (to 23.8 per cent in 1984). There was additionally a numerical rise of this household type, by about 2 million. For Spanish origin families there has been a stable poverty rate, at about 17 per cent for male-headed homes, and 53 per cent for female-headed homes (from 1972 to 1984) but the number of the latter has doubled to 905,000. The picture then is closer to the white than the black pattern, but the poverty rates generally higher.

The feminisation of poverty thus refers to two different phenomena. One is the general increase across the population of household types which tend to experience poverty. This group includes both elderly and non-elderly women living alone, though by far the largest category is the lone mother household, which experiences a much higher rate of poverty than the rest of the population, and has also grown in number. The proportion of the poor population living in this kind of arrangement has rocketed, and so 'female heads' are carrying a disproportionate burden of the country's poverty. For the black population the feminisation of poverty has an additional dimension in that other household types have experienced reductions in poverty rates while·single mothers have experienced increases. The benefit which had originally been designed to allow lone mothers (notably widows) to support children was the focus of criticism for encouraging unbridled and irresponsible sexual indulgence (cf. Malthus), though Harrington notes that for the 1970s at least, among single mothers family size was close to the average. Bane (1988: 384) reports that:

> An analysis of the reasons for the increased feminization of poverty suggests that about 40 per cent of the increase is accounted for by changes in relative poverty rates and about 60 per cent by changes in population composition. Changes in relative poverty rates were considerably more important for blacks than whites.

Competing moral judgements are embodied in the interpretation of this data:

1 Society is pushing responsibility for its poverty on to a vulnerable population of lone mothers.
2 Women are forced to carry the family burden of high levels of male unemployment.
3 Society in its affluence has encouraged irresponsible behaviour among women.
4 Welfare encourages irresponsible behaviour among men, who can avoid the responsibilities of fatherhood and employment.
5 The women concerned fail in their task of socialisation and reproduce the pattern in the next generation.

Bane (1988) addresses the problem of explanation which underlies these judgements and focuses on the transition to female-headed households. She first argues (on the basis of data from three-generational households) that the circumstances of the parents' families of origin suggests that 20 per cent of white children born to unmarried mothers and 50 per cent of black children born to unmarried mothers would have been poor even if the parents had married. The feminisation of poverty is thus argued to be two different problems: 'One of mostly temporary poverty for women whose poverty follows directly from a family change (i.e. marital breakup), and one of mostly chronic poverty for women who came from situations that offer opportunities for neither men nor women' (p. 385).

Comment on the feminisation of poverty has sometimes been viewed in the context of the maintenance of male dominance and female dependence and couched in terms of patriarchy (e.g. Moran, 1985), although this concept is generally conceded to carry its own problems (see Bradley, 1989). Certainly the traditional household arrangement of male breadwinner and female housewife has been fundamentally challenged by deteriorating employment opportunities for many men, and by the increased entry into the labour force of married women. Women's disadvantage extends beyond their association with the domestic role, however, to the way in which traditional perceptions of women's role and the organisation of paid work condemn many to a weak position in the labour market (see Morris, 1990 for review). Lone mothers in the States find themselves the object of mounting but conflicting pressures. On the one hand the traditional household structure is defended against the alleged failure of the lone mother to adequately fulfil her role as agent of morality and socialisation. On the other she is exhorted to join the trend in which mothers are increasingly active members of the labour force.

ROLE CONFLICT

When AFDC was introduced in 1935 it was to enable lone mothers (predominantly widows) to maintain their children without going to work. Increasingly the policy trend is towards some means of work enforcement for welfare recipients. It might seem that the very low level of subsistence supported by AFDC would be sufficient inducement, for as Ellwood (1987) has reported, in 1987 none of the states offered combined support from AFDC and food stamps which reached the poverty line. Furthermore, up until 1962 earnings were deducted dollar for dollar from benefit. In 1962 a work expenses disregard, including child care costs, was introduced, and in 1967 an earnings disregard exempted the first $30 per month from earnings, plus one-third of the remaining earnings after work expenses (Brown, 1989). In the same year WIN (Work Incentive Program) registration became compulsory for claimants with children aged six or over, and offered job search and training services.

A more brutal approach was adopted in the 1981 legislation which withdrew the disregard, reduced the work expenses allowance and placed a ceiling on child care costs, as well as allowing states the option of introducing Workfare programmes whereby AFDC recipients would be required to engage in upaid work to the value of their benefit. The programmes could be extended to mothers of children aged 3–5 as long as child care costs were met. The legislation has two purposes: to end the use of AFDC as a supplement to low pay by allowing generous disregards, and to enforce a work requirement. In fact only four states opted to operate Workfare on a statewide basis, though they tended to exempt those with high child care costs (Brown, 1989: 67). Gueron (1988) reports on the impact of eight Workfare programmes, which were found to produce small increases in employment: participants in San Diego showed an employment rate of 61 per cent, as against 55 per cent employment for the control group. 'Changes occur, but the evidence does not suggest that the programs examined up to now offer an immediate solution to the problems of poverty and dependency. Income and employment do increase, but the changes are not dramatic' (Gueron, 1988: 23).

Brown (1989), however, also cites the statements from the Congressional Budget Office noting the failure to assess the impact of the programmes on the children concerned and asserting that 'single women with children who have not yet started school are already contributing to society by caring for their children. . . . Society has a strong interest in ensuring that the children are properly cared for' (pp. 71–2). Finally, the possible displacement effect whereby Workfare actually reduced standard employment, and the very low quality of employment which successful participants found, have also been remarked upon. Brown cites the Committee of Ways and Means' observation that 'Their increased earnings are often not large enough to raise them above the poverty line, although they reduce the severity of their poverty' (1985, in Brown, 1989: 538).

This pushes the conceptualisation of the underclass away from narrowly confined notions of the work ethic and issues of sexual morality and towards the construction of the labour market, and the confinement of some potential workers to a position which is insufficient for reasonable maintenance. This issue connects with the British debate about definitions of the underclass, cited in the previous chapter, and has also been taken up by Jencks (1992:

204): 'Single mothers do not turn to welfare because they are pathologically dependent on handouts or unusually reluctant to work – they do so because they cannot get jobs that pay better than welfare.' He argues that this forces many welfare dependent women into undeclared work and fraudulent claiming, citing evidence from a series of intensive interviews with 25 welfare families in an area with welfare payments close to the national average. His conclusions are also supported by reference to the Consumer Expenditure Survey. 'An unskilled single mother cannot expect to support herself and her children in today's labour market either by working or by collecting welfare. . . . Her best hope . . . is to collect AFDC and to work without telling the welfare department' (cited in Jencks, 1992: 204).

He argues that the fraud is deemed to be justified in terms of a morality which sees reasonable provision for children as a priority, and which therefore denies the moral legitimacy of the inadequate welfare system; a system 'incompatible with everyday American morality' (p. 205). Welfare recipients do not lie and cheat (if they do) because they are part of a deviant sub-culture, Jencks argues, but because it is their only means of achieving subsistence standards. To ensure that a single mother could keep herself and her children, would mean raising the minimum wage at a time when there is already an excess of unskilled labour. As we saw in Chapter 3 it has been argued by many that a high rate of unemployment for men is the true reason for increased single motherhood. As it stands, welfare has simply created a system which makes it impossible for single mothers to improve their situation by working harder, and in this it 'violates deeply held American ideals' (Jencks, 1992: 228).

Jencks thus frames his analysis in terms of the constraints of employment opportunities and the economic structure, and also as a process of rational decision making, guided by certain moral priorities. The counter-argument emphasises problem values and behaviour and sees a solution as lying in personal responsibility and social obligation (Novak, 1987). The two planks of the latter approach would be the enforcement of fathers' child-support obligations and the imposition of Workfare programmes on all single mothers. The other logical step is to extend AFDC to include families with an unemployed father present, and this was in fact achieved in the 1988 Family Support Act, with the condition of 16 hours' work per week in government jobs. Such provision

comes closer to the pro-family argument which supports traditional gender roles and sees any impositon of Workfare upon
mothers as an assault on the value of the family (Gilder, 1987).

THE BRITISH CASE

In Britain the system of welfare provision differs from that of the
States and has always made provision for an unemployed man with
a family, albeit at poverty levels. Nevertheless, the changes in
family structure which have been documented in America appear
to be under way here, with single parent families growing from 8
per cent of all families with children in 1971, to 16 per cent in 1988
(Brown, 1990: 43). The principal reason for single motherhood in
Britain is divorce, which accounted for 40 per cent of single
mothers in 1986, with separation accounting for 19 per cent, and
never-married mothers accounting for 23 per cent. This last
percentage has risen from 15 per cent in 1972. Ten per cent of
single parents in 1986 were men (Brown, 1989). It is the disproportionately rapid growth of the never-married category of single
mothers which has prompted comparison with the US (Murray,·
1990). The two countries also have in common increasing rates of
divorce and a growing percentage of children born out of wedlock,
although often in cohabiting unions. There are, however, points
of difference to be noted.

Although there is a high concentration of single parents within
the black population, notably 31 per cent of West Indian households with children in 1984 as compared with 10 per cent for the
white population and 5 per cent for Asians, the total non-white
population in Britain is only 5.5 per cent (1991 census, London,
OPCS). British single parents are thus overwhelmingly white. A
further contrast is that in Britain single mothers leave single
parenthood much sooner than divorced mothers, with a median
duration of 35 months, as compared with 59 months for divorced
mothers in that status (Ermisch, 1986). Fifty-five per cent of single
parents in the UK are regular benefit claimants, but the duration
of benefit dependence tends to be longer for divorced mothers
than for single mothers. Of the latter group Ermisch (1986) found
that 60 per cent of those who entered this status with the birth of
a child will have left it by the time the child is five years old, and
70 per cent by the time the child is seven.

On balance, it would seem that there is even less of a case for arguing that the growth in lone parenthood is strongly associated with the growth of an underclass in Britain than in the US. Lone parenthood is less common than in the US, though growing in both places, a lower proportion of lone parents is made up of never-married women, only a minority become long term benefit dependent, and the proportion is higher among divorced mothers than among single mothers. There are signs, however, that duration of dependence has grown with worsening economic conditions. In 1981, of those on benefit, 7.8 per cent of single mothers and 9.6 per cent of divorced mothers had been claiming for more than ten years, with 23 per cent of single mothers and 27 per cent of divorced mothers claiming for five years or more. By 1987 the figure for single mothers had risen to 27 per cent, with divorced mothers remaining stable (Brown, 1990).

The same underlying issues of gender role conflict are revealed in Smith's (1992) commentary on the Policy Studies Institute conference on the British underclass. I quote selectively from his conclusions:

> the proposed minimalist definition of the underclass, in terms of detachment from the labour market, assumes that the traditional family is the norm . . . non-working women with working husbands do not fall into the underclass, because their family unit is integrated into the labour market. On the other hand, non-working lone mothers do normally fall within the underclass. . . . Yet if the endorsement of the traditional family turns on the importance of child-rearing, it is a paradox that lone mothers define themselves out of the underclass only if they get themselves a job instead of devoting themselves to rearing their children. . . . They are given a choice between two evils: staying at home to look after their children, in which case they become part of an underclass; or going out to work, in which case they are failing to sustain an ideal of motherhood that others seek to impose. (p. 92)

This is an example of what Roche (1992: 152), in relation to US policy debates, terms a conflict between a work ethic and a family ethic. Indeed, much of the British policy debate on single mothers concerns why they do not, in larger numbers, enter paid employment; this in the context of a national labour market in which about 70 per cent of married women are employed. However, as Brown points out, almost 50 per cent of married women with dependent children are not in paid work, as compared with roughly 60 per cent of lone mothers. Various sources (Martin and Roberts, 1984; *Social Trends*, General Household Survey) have demonstrated that the real difference occurs in participation in part time work. Thus in 1986, 7 per cent of married mothers of under-fives were working full time and 9 per cent of lone mothers, whilst fewer lone mothers than married mothers work part time. In interpreting these figures we should note that 60 per cent of the children of lone parents were under five years old, and that 74 per cent of married women with a child under five did not take work in 1982–4, 43 per cent of those with a youngest child aged 5–9, and 31 per cent of those with children aged 10 or over (*Social Trends*, 1986).

In part these figures reflect the greater difficulties of providing care for younger children, but they are also linked to the still strong feelings many women have about their maternal duties, and what is best for their children. For example, the Women and Employment Survey of 1980 found that '60 per cent of women thought that the mother of a pre-school child "ought to stay at home", and a further 25 per cent thought "she should only go out to work if she really needs the money". For school age children, the figures were much lower, but still quite substantial – 11 per cent "she ought to stay at home" and 36 per cent she should work only if "she really needs the money"' (cited in Brown, 1989: 21).

This, of course poses for lone parents the dilemma set out by Smith above, or in Roche's terms poses the family ethic against and above the work ethic.

WHY DON'T THEY GO TO WORK?

The title of this section is taken from the excellent review by Joan Brown (1989), upon which I draw heavily here. As we have seen, one central issue linking single mothers to the underclass concerns the alleged lack of socialisation into mainstream values, though oddly one of the reasons Brown gives for the lesser engagement of lone mothers in paid work is the impact of social conditioning which requires a mother to be with her children when they are very young. The other underclass connection concerns the assumed absence of a work ethic among those who are benefit dependent. There is a tension here for single mothers between their mothering role and the increasing expectation that they should be employed.

Brown (1989) reviews the evidence other than social conditioning which might explain why some are not.

Research into the wishes of lone mothers with regard to employment shows that the overwhelming majority would like employment, provided good care for their children was ensured. There was 89 per cent agreement on the statements 'If her children are well looked after it's good for a woman to work', 'The social security system should give more help to lone mothers who want to work', and 'Child care facilities for lone mothers ought to be improved to enable them to work' (Weale *et al.*, 1984). These statements assume greater significance when set against the actual working patterns of women with children. About half of all working mothers in 1985 worked less than 20 hours per week. Furthermore, the *Women and Employment* survey (Martin and Roberts, 1984) found that a vital element in the child care arrangements of working mothers was the husband; for 50 per cent of mothers with pre-school children and 63 per cent of those with school age children. The survey also reported that the great majority of women returning to work after having children were seeking part time work. Women with dependent children were more likely to work part time than women without (35 per cent as against 6 per cent part time, 17 per cent as against 78 per cent full time), and married women were more likely than single women to do so (33 per cent as against 3 per cent part time, and 27 per cent as against 79 per cent full time).

The corollary of this of course is that many married women are working for a secondary wage: although the money they earn is vital for household maintenance, it would not be sufficient alone to provide for the household needs, and is certainly a lower amount than that earned by their husbands. There is a corresponding pattern in changes in the labour market throughout the 1980s. This period has not only seen a rise in the proportion of married women in paid employment, there has also been a gradual shift away from full time and towards part time work for women. Part time work was the only sustained area of job growth throughout the 1980s (though this aggregate figure disguises some part time losses from manufacturing in the early 1980s).

So many married women with dependent children not only are secondary earners, they are in secondary employment: work that is low paid, insecure, and designed for cheapness and disposability. Part time workers get fewer employment rights, lesser protection, and below a specified wage ceiling per week do not pay National Insurance contributions. The effect is to make their employment cheaper for employers, but to debar them from claiming unemployment benefit on the loss of their job. This at last brings us back to the concept of the underclass, and the conceptual discussion in Chapter 4. If we define the underclass in terms of long term dependence on benefit, then single parents cannot but be included. The definition could, however, be broadened, as in the definition considered by Gallie (1988), to include those systematically disadvantaged in the labour market. In this case the part time work of married women would surely qualify them, although their household circumstances might not warrant their inclusion.

The fact that part time work has been the principal area of employment growth for women, especially at the low-skilled end of the spectrum, may pose a problem for lone mothers. The earnings rule for Income Support claimants (previously Supplementary Benefit) has never been generous. There has, however, been an increase to £15 per week, as of 1988, after which a full deduction of earnings applies. No allowance is made for work expenses, even child care. This means that earnings which do not substantially exceed the level of benefits are unlikely to be of much use to the mother. Given the general dearth of state-provided full time child care provision, the very high cost of private care, and the absence of a husband to provide such care, part time work for single parents is not a viable option, though it is the work most readily available for unskilled women. On the other hand, full time work means a much greater commitment of time away from chidren than a single parent feels able to give, and unless the pay is relatively good the mother will find that child care costs leave her worse off than when claiming Income Support. 'The prospects for a lone mother with a child under five to support herself and her child through work, without other income or subsidies are poor. Indeed she has limited chances of working at all' (Brown, 1989: 36). Is she therefore part of an underclass? The term seems inadequate to capture the complexity of constraints under which she operates, particularly when it carries strong implications of moral failure.

SOCIAL POLARISATION

Before we leave discussion of the relationship between the benefit system and women's labour market position we should give some attention to one aspect of what has been termed social polarisation: the process whereby opportunities for work have been concentrated in some homes but absent from others. If the underclass is to be defined as Smith (1992) suggests, in terms of the household and by the absence of any secure link with the labour market, then we must consider the situation whereby the wives of unemployed men are predominantly out of work themselves. On what basis should unemployed men whose wives are not employed be termed an underclass, whilst those whose wives are working are not? Social polarisation is much debated in Britain, whilst US discussion focuses much more on receipt of AFDC recipients, yet the American situation is not unlike the British one; the wives of unemployed men tend themselves to be out of work (see Morris, 1990).

This has been the case in Britain at least since 1973 when 34 per cent of the wives of unemployed men were employed themselves, as compared with 55 per cent of the wives of employed men. This gap widened consistently until 1985 when the percentages were respectively 22 per cent and 62 per cent. The figures since show a rise in the employment rates of both groups of women, but with the gap still widening. The 1987 figures were 27 per cent and 69 per cent respectively. A study of men unemployed in 1978 found that a difference was apparent only one month into the man's unemployment, but that the difference grew with duration of unemployment. Of particular significance, however, was the 12-month point at which the men moved off (contributory) Unemployment Benefit (UB) and on to (means tested) Supplementary Benefit (SB: now Income Support: IS). The calculation of permitted earnings is different for the two benefits, and in effect employment for a spouse is much more worthwhile when claiming UB than SB (or IS). The percentage of wives in employment fell from 32 per cent one month after registration to 22 per cent twelve months on. The more generous earnings rules for spouses of claimants of UB have been seen as an obvious explanation, and several other studies have called attention to this possibility.

Work by Dilnot and Kell (1989) offers examples of the gain from a spouse's employment both for UB and SB (IS), taking all other benefits into account. Their conclusion is that for women whose husbands are on UB there is a significant deterrent to part time work, other than for a few hours a week, but not to full time work. And in fact the data for 1984 show that those women who worked at all were much more likely to work full time. In the case of the means tested benefit, however, employment for a spouse was deemed 'fundamentally incompatible', and it was judged reasonable that almost 90 per cent of wives were not employed in 1984. Another study which interviewed couples about their decisions (McLaughlin *et al.*, 1989) found that the disincentive embodied in low disregards was commonly cited as a reason for the non-employment of the wife, that the woman was more likely to be employed if the couple had no children and/or were in the early stages of the man's unemployment. Again a critical point was found to be the transition from UB to SB (IS).

This account is contested by some, however. Joshi (1984: 25) has run through a number of reasons for an association of unemployment between husband and wife, which for women may include an increased domestic burden as a result of the man's presence in the home, a wish to share time together, or a reluctance to usurp the breadwinner role. Men's resistance to this possibility has been noted in other studies (Morris, 1985; Bell and McKee, 1985), whilst a number of writers suggest that the disincentive effect has been exaggerated. Analysis of DHSS cohort data (Moylan *et al.*, 1984) found that this effect accounted for only a small part of the reduced probability of the wives' employment (cf. Davies *et al.*, 1991). Other possible factors included the state of the local economy, low skill levels for husband and wife, prohibition of the wife's employment by the husband, or reluctance to seek employment by the wife (cf. Morris, 1985).

Recent work by Irwin and Morris (1993) has taken up the apparent disparity between accounts of the experience of couples on benefit, noting that data from wives of unemployed men in the north-east of England show that only 12 per cent explain their non-employment by reference to benefit regulations. Comparisons between this group and the wives of both securely and insecurely employed men show a range of differences. The commonest reason for leaving jobs among the women were pregnancy, family or health reasons, and redundancy, the latter category being slightly more common for the wives of employed men, and pregnancy etc., for the wives of unemployed men. The wives of unemployed men were more likely to have young children in the home, but also more likely to cite child care as a reason for not working than other women in the same familial situation. One reason here is the difference between skill levels and prospects for the different groups of women. The wives of unemployed men tend to be less skilled, have poorer prospects, and be candidates for less rewarding work, than the wives of employed men. They are also more vulnerable to unemployment in their own right. This to a great extent mirrors the position of their husbands.

It is this combination of factors, rather than male employment per se, or the direct and unitary effect of the benefit regulations, which offers the fullest explanation of the concentration of male and female unemployment within households. Even confining ourselves to the disincentive effect, a full understanding requires an examination not only of benefit rulings but of their interaction with married women's position in the labour market. Unless a woman can earn substantially more than the household can claim in benefit, she will be to some degree deterred from earning at all. It is therefore the disadvantaged position and poor prospects of the majority of married women which mean that a wife is unlikely to become a sole earner. The growing concentration of part time employment among married women makes such an outcome even less probable.

GENDER AND WORK

So in Britain at least the issue of non-employment for women is not addressed predominantly in terms of the position of single parents, as tends to be the case in the US, but rather through the low levels of unemployment among the wives of unemployed men, i.e. the concentration of unemployment within households. What links the two debates is the status of benefit dependence, and this, as we have seen, is the basis of at least one definition of the 'underclass'. However, it would seem that this term is inadequate to capture the complexities which lie behind the employment experience of women married to unemployed men. Whilst a number of writers have emphasised that the household is the appropriate unit for the examination of social exclusion and/or non-participation in the labour market, this still leaves a number of gender related issues unexamined.

One feature of Murray's conception of the underclass concerns the absence of a work incentive. It is not clear that the non-employment of married women can be properly viewed from this perspective, despite a generally increased female participation in the workforce. Although a substantial amount of material shows that the lack of financial reward has featured in the

disproportionately low employment levels of the wives of unemployed men, we have found other complicating factors. Some are
directly linked to gender issues, such as reluctance to challenge the
man's breadwinner role, responsibilities to young children, and
vulnerability in the labour market, this latter point being linked
to the other two. Certainly women at the lower end of the
employment spectrum, as the wives of unemployed men tend to
be, are likely to find their employment prospects structured
around the assumption that theirs is a secondary wage, and this is
particularly true of part time work, the main growth area of
employment for women.

The most compelling reason for women's failure to take over as
principal breadwinners is their poor earning capacity, which of
course acts to reinforce gendered assumptions about their appropriate role (see Morris, 1987). This raises again the issue of
definition of an 'underclass'. As we saw in Chapter 4, the broadest
approach to the definition of the underclass includes all those
chronically disadvantaged in the labour market, and this would
include a good many women workers. The fact that the majority
of this group, notably the part time employees, are married to men
in employment has been argued, on the grounds of *household*
circumstances, to remove them from the designation 'underclass'
(Gallie, 1988). On the other hand, it is the fact that the wives of
unemployed men are not supported by another income which
prevents them from taking employment with earnings inadequate
for household maintenance. The notion of an underclass defined
by dependency is of little use in guiding us through an explanation
of non-employment and labour market disadvantage for women
which stems from gender related issues. Pressures derived from
gender roles are not, however, confined to women.

The importance of the 'breadwinner' role for men and the
challenge that unemployment poses to gender identity is one of
the strongest arguments against the suggestion that a culture of
dependency underlies high levels of long term unemployment. A
recent study by Jordan *et al.* (1992) is based on interviews with a
mix of unemployed, securely employed and insecurely employed
male workers and their wives. The major limitation of the study
and the reported conclusions is the fact that the sample included
only eleven unemployed men, and this is too small a number for
generalisation, especially given the contentious nature of some of
the authors' assertions. One point which is made repeatedly, and

which has also emerged from other studies (Morris, 1985; Davies and Ritchie, 1988), is the importance of work as a source of male identity, the other side of which is a constraint on women's assumption of the breadwinner role. Male respondents stressed the boredom and lack of meaning in a life without work: 'The men described themselves as active, needing to work to fulfil their personal needs as well as their roles as providers for their households. Idleness is characterised as boring and destructive of identity and self respect' (Jordan et al., 1992: 99).

This need for work, together with the inadeqate income which derives from benefit, pushed a number of men into undeclared work, which was justified in terms of an obligation to meet the family's 'extra' needs. This is one aspect of the findings about which I feel reservations. Other research (Morris, 1990; 1991) shows that by no means all unemployed men are in receipt of illicit earnings, and Jordan's sample is nowhere near large enough to warrant the assertions he makes. The occasional opportunity for casual work is something reported by a number of researchers (see Chapter 4) and as in Jordan's study it is commonly reported that the administrative problems of declaring such casual earnings is a considerable deterrent from doing so. Jordan argues that opportunities for informal work are 'Constructed as a legitimate way of getting out of administrative traps which frustrate the active worker who wants to be a successful breadwinner' (Jordan et al., 1992: 125). In other words the behaviour is legitimised in terms of dominant values. More generally, however, Jordan makes the point that the men 'Constructed their identities as frustrated workers, rather than satisfied beneficiaries – as victims of an unemployment trap, not as voluntary unemployed' (p. 123).

In this respect there is something in common between the position of the wives of unemployed men or single mothers, and that of unskilled, unemployed male workers; both have to consider how the wages on offer compare to the income derived from benefit. Part of the emphasis on male identity being tied to the breadwinner role is the capacity to earn sufficient to keep a family, and a recurrent theme of research findings is the degradation of working for a wage which is not adequate to meet these needs. To accept an inadequate wage and claim additional benefits available as Family Credit is seen by many of the working population as a challenge to dignity: 'It's degrading a man . . . to work for that wage' (Jordan et al., 1992: 121; cf. Morris, 1987), though we have already noted that assertions of acceptable wage levels are un-reliable, many people being prepared to work for less when an opportunity arises (McLaughlin *et al.*, 1989). Take-up of in-work benefit is notoriously low, however, at about 55 per cent of eligible claimants (Morris, 1991).

One last point to be made about gender related issues and the underclass, which connects with the literature on the feminisation of poverty, is that there is a good deal of research which argues that women bear a particular burden in absorbing the household impact of the social phenomenon to which the notion of an 'underclass' refers. Either through their sole responsibility for the household, in the case of single mothers, or through their budget-ing and catering role in the presence of an unemployed man, women are affected in specific ways by household benefit depen-dence. By virtue of their traditional association with the domestic sphere the task of managing an inadequate budget falls to women, often at the cost of friction with their spouse (Morris, 1984, 1990).

THE FAMILY AND THE UNDERCLASS

In every request for aid, one had to locate and bring to light the moral fault that more or less directly determined it; that portion of neglectfulness, laziness, and dissolution that every instance of misery contained. In this new policy, morality was systematically linked to the economic factor, involving a continuous surveillance of the family. (Donzelot, 1979: 69)

This statement was made with reference to France at the break-up of feudalism, when the family came to have a key role in the preservation of social order, by caring for those unable to provide for themselves, and by instilling the values of industry. In the family lay the state's solution to the problems of pauperism and the means of discipline for the working class, through the inter-mediary of philanthropy. Relief, however, was required to serve in some manner in the rehabilitation of the family. Welfare as a moralising force, and the family as the vehicle of morality, are both evident in different ways in the sprawling literature on the underclass.

Much discussion of the policy problems and recommendations about the underclass are cast in terms of debate about 'the family'. By this what is usually meant is the nuclear family household, in which, by tradition at least, the man has the principal bread-winning role and the mother the nurturing role of socialisation. This, of course, represents the Parsonian view of the 'modern' family in which the fit with industrial society is achieved by just such specialised gender roles. It is the model which underlies much early policy thinking in both Britain and America. In part the dilemma of the wives of unemployed men in the UK stems from this foundation. Beveridge, the principal architect of the British welfare state, took the view that women wanted social insurance 'for others, not for themselves'. He argued that: 'the ideal social unit is the household of man, wife and children maintained by the earnings of the first alone. . . . Reasonable security of employ-ment for the breadwinner is the basis of all private duties and all sound social action', and that: 'The great majority of married women must be regarded as occupied on work which is vital though unpaid, without which their husbands could not do their paid work and without which the nation could not continue' (both quoted in Land, 1980).

As noted earlier, AFDC was introduced in 1935 as a benefit principally intended for widows, to enable them to support and care for their children without taking paid work:

> to release from the wage earning role the person whose natural function is to give her children the physical and affectionate guardianship necessary not alone to keep them from falling into misfortune, but more affirmatively to rear them into citizens capable of contributing to society. (In CBO, 1987: 7)

The expectation was that the need for this benefit would be gradually eliminated with growing eligibility for social security (by virtue of the husband's contributions: the increasing dependence upon the provision by lone parents was never foreseen. In this sense the traditional 'family' was taken for granted. At a time when married mothers are increasingly active in the workforce there is debate in both Britain and America about the expectations which can properly be imposed upon lone mothers. In the absence of a father, do they become the exemplars of the work ethic?

> Our support for better working opportunities for lone parents is not based on the view that they ought to be supporting themselves. Many lone parents believe that it is better to concentrate their efforts on the difficult and important task of

bringing up children single handed, and they are entitled to do that. (SBC, 1979)

Concern about a developing 'underclass' is principally a concern about the failure of sections of the male population of Britain and America to fulfil the breadwinning role, but the family and therefore women are implicated by virtue of their responsibility for socialisation. One dimension of academic debate turns upon the question of causation, and whether understanding is to be found in structural or behavioural explanations of unemployment (see Chapter 4). Another takes the behavioural approach as common ground but disagrees about the proper role of the family in the inculcation of appropriate values and behaviour. Roche (1992) has identified a key controversy within the neo-conservative approach to welfare in the US, which embodies a debate about the balance between work duty and family duty, and with it a debate about changing gender roles.

Novak's (1987) policy emphasis is upon 'helping the family', which he sees to be threatened by paternal desertion and/or marital break-up. Both high rates of unemployment and a falling rate of marriage for black youth are stressed, with passing reference to the need for economic growth. For Novak, however, the problems of the 'underclass' may be traced back to 'behavioural dependence'. The inculcation of social responsibility is argued to be vital, and particularly paternal responsibility for children. In Novak's view there should also be deterrents to teenage pregnancy, however, such as the denial of support for an independent household for mothers under 18, making AFDC temporary, and above all enforcing a work obligation as a condition of welfare. There is a clear acknowledgement that even in the presence of an employed father the mother's wage may be necessary to keep the family out of poverty.

Gilder's view, in contrast, opposes a role in paid work for women. For him the aim of policy should be to 'restore work and family as instruments of male socialisation among the poor' (1986:195). The existing welfare system in the States is argued to deregulate sexuality (i.e. reproduction), and in doing so to deprive black families of their fathers. For Gilder the imposition of work obligations on single mothers only exacerbates the problem. These women are already 'incapable of taming teenage boys', and to impose on them the obligation of paid employment will 'accelerate family decay' (p. 21). An extension of state-provided child support is his preferred solution, the benefit which Beveridge introduced to Britain through Family Allowance as a support for the working population. Ironically, this is a solution which would be supported by many feminists, who see some form of child support as essentially a support for mothers, and one which diminishes their dependence on the man's disposal of his earnings.

While close to Gilder in some ways the Bergers (1983) come to a rather different conclusion. The 'bourgeois family' is seen by the Bergers as a foundation of democracy and as the best means of socialising young citizens. For them it is under threat by the increasing pursuit of self-gratification, by destructive sexual mores, and by the expanding entry of married women into the workforce. Support for sole mothers is seen as an inappropriate policy response to the fragility of traditional domestic arrangements. This touches on a key issue for feminist thinking on the role of state support: whether to seek provisions for women which will enhance their traditional role, or whether to challenge the validity of traditional arrangements between the sexes. Raised tangentially by the debate about an emergent 'underclass', these issues lie at the heart of conceptualisations of women's citizenship.

WOMEN AND CITIZENSHIP

'While Marshall asserts the rights of citizenship, nowhere does he analyse the problematic relationship between citizenship and dependency in the family as he does between citizenship and social class' (Pascall, 1986: 9). Held (1989: 173) makes a similar point: 'To analyse citizenship as if it were a matter of the exclusion or inclusion of social classes is to eclipse from view a variety of dimensions of social life which have been central to the struggle over citizenship.' One of the neglected dimensions he identifies is the position of women.

The social security system which emerged from the Beveridge plan, and which Marshall saw as one of the main guarantors of citizenship for all, was in fact based upon the assumption of married women's dependence: 'The status of married women as dependants has often been entrenched by the very "social rights" that are seen as the final crown of citizenship' (Pascall, 1986: 9). This is the central plank of what Pateman (1989) terms the patriarchal welfare state. In liberal democracy the concern to guarantee equality in civic life has been confined to the public domain, and as Dietz (1987) argues, the very concept of rights (and certainly social rights) is a public one. The ideal of citizenship is then based upon a distinction between public and private spheres, but in a society where the public and the private are gendered spheres. Held (1989: 175) immediately highlights a problem for women when he argues that:

> To unpack the domain of rights is to unpack both the rights citizens formally enjoy and the conditions under which citizens' rights are actually realised and enacted. Only this 'double focus' makes it possible to grasp the degrees of autonomy, inter-dependence and constraint that citizens face in the societies in which they live.

The status and autonomy of women have been undermined by their association with the private sphere and by the operations of the very mechanism designed to guarantee universal social rights. One early suggested solution was an endowment for motherhood in the form of a child benefit (cf. Gilder, 1986). This was supported by Eleanor Rathbone on the basis that:

> There is perhaps no relation in life as it is lived in a modern industrial community where the temptations to selfishness are greater and checks on it fewer than the relationship between a wage-earning husband and a wholly dependent wife. (Quoted in Lister, 1989: 6)

Lister (citing Land, 1980 and Graham, 1987) goes on to argue that the absence of enforceable rights to a portion of a husband's income can put some women in an untenable situation where dependency on means-tested benefit from the state may be preferable, though this now carries the stigmatising label of 'underclass'. For Dietz (1987: 13) the danger of bolstering women's traditional position is the tendency 'to turn historically distinctive women into ahistorical, universalised entities'. Following a similar line of argument Pateman identifies a dilemma central to women's early claims to citizenship; either they insist that as women they have specific capacities and needs, or they demand their incorporation into some 'gender-neutral' ideal (1989: 196).

Recent developments in the conceptualisation of citizenship have increasingly placed at least as much emphasis on obligations as on rights, the prime obligation being work as a means to independence (cf. Pateman). This places women in an ambiguous position; either they earn their 'public' citizenship rights by their own paid employment, or they perform their 'private' family obligations and remain dependent. This conflict can only be resolved by a redistribution of the 'private' obligations of unpaid labour, or by some acknowledgement of the 'public' service such labour performs, or by increasing state involvement in the 'private' obligation to care for children. The current situation, however, leaves individual women in something of a dilemma, especially if the fathers of their children are unwilling or unable to fulfil *their* traditional role. These women, according to Pateman (1989), become the new 'undeserving poor', disadvantaged in a labour market which is structured around the assumption that women's employment is secondary. This dilemma equally affects married women with employed husbands, who are faced with strongly held beliefs about 'appropriate' gender roles and whose inferior earning capacity leaves them inadequate as sole earners.

Despite competing definitions of the 'underclass', state dependence and non-employment have played a central role in debate. Instead of guaranteeing social inclusion welfare dependence is increasingly seen as a badge of inadequacy. The dilemma for women stems from the fact that the welfare state in both Britain and America rests upon a traditional conceptualisation of domestic organisation and gender roles in which women are *necessarily* dependants. There have been changes in the operation of the benefit system both in Britain and the US. For example in Britain either the woman or the man can opt to claim on behalf of the couple, while in America families with an unemployed father are now eligible for AFDC. Furthermore, many single mothers face work requirements as a condition of welfare. However, beliefs about appropriate gender roles remain strong in both countries (see Morris, 1990) and women's inferior position in the labour market makes any real challenge to traditional role expectations difficult. As I have argued elsewhere (Morris, 1990), it is the interaction of statutory, economic and ideological constraints which is so powerful in inhibiting any renegotiation of gender relations.

For single parents the dilemma identified by Pateman is particularly clear. As benefit dependants they are stigmatised members of the 'underclass', and as such are failing in their distinctively 'female' role of socialising the next generation. It is argued that the children in such households suffer from the absence of a breadwinning role model, and yet the weak position of the majority of sole mothers in the labour market prevents them from easily assuming this role themselves. Even were they to do so this would raise the problem of child care, and more generally of whether they were meeting their traditional obligations as a mother. One response to this complex of problems has been strongly to reaffirm the strengths of traditional arrangements, as in the Bergers' *The War Over the Family* (1983). Novak (1987) offers an alternative view which recognises the possible need for two incomes, but a more radical alternative states that any solution to the impasse over women's rights to social inclusion can only be achieved by a fundamental and far reaching review of many taken-for-granted aspects of social life:

> If women as well as men are to be full citizens, the separation of the welfare state and employment from the free welfare work contributed by women has to be broken down and new meanings and practices of 'independence', 'work', and 'welfare' created. (Pateman, 1989: 202)

Chapter 6

Migrant labour and the underclass

This last substantive chapter raises an issue which has been indirectly present in much of the discussion so far: that of the nature and degree of integration of 'outsiders' into a given socio-political unit. Part of this process rests, of course, upon the social construction of the category. The distrust awakened by the 'stranger' was apparent in popular responses to migrant labour in eighteenth-century England, with settlement regulations designed to protect parishes against the costs of the wandering poor; each parish was prepared to be responsible only for its 'own' population. The assumptions implicit here are that the members of any given community are accountable for the generation and deployment of the resources of that community, and must protect them from the illegitimate demands of 'outsiders'. The issue becomes heated when the outsiders are most easily identifiable as such, as for example with the Irish and Jewish population of nineteenth-century London, though we also saw in Chapter 1 examples of how the poor could be constructed as a race apart *by virtue of* their poverty. It may indeed be true that the availability of resources affects the decision to migrate, and this has been argued in the case of southern blacks in the US, whose home states offered minimal, if any, welfare support. We also noted, however, that this population was not quite the drain on the welfare systems of the North that it was popularly supposed to be. Where migration occurs across national boundaries these issues are all the more salient, and necessarily involve questions of citizenship and the social rights that follow from citizenship.

I have previously referred to the seminal work of T.H. Marshall and his conceptualisation of citizenship as 'full membership of a community', for purposes of civil, political and social rights and duties. Yuval-Davis takes up this point and problematises the notion of 'community':

> It assumes a given collectivity . . . [not] an ideological and material construction, whose boundaries, structures and norms are a result of constant processes of struggles and negotiations, or more general social developments. Any dynamic notion of citizenship must start from the processes which construct the collectivity. (1990: 3)

The obvious example concerns the circumstances and conditions of migration across socio-political boundaries, the place of the new arrival in the social and economic structures of the receiving 'community', and the rights of this individual to the resources and protections the 'community' conventionally offers to its citizens. The acceptance of migrant labour is often designed to be partial, to take the labour without conferring the rights of membership. Carens (1988) has considered the philosophical roots of such issues in the context of Mexican migration into the United States, though a topical and interesting case of the negotiation and renegotiation of these matters also arises in relation to migration into the European Community.

'The conventional moral view is that a country is justified in restricting immigration whenever it serves the national interest to do so' (Carens, 1988: 207). The question commonly arises in contemporary society in relation to concern about accelerating demands upon the welfare state. The usual fear is that large scale immigration will undermine the will and the capacity to support the institutions of the welfare state. However:

> Almost all of the illegal immigrants and many of the legal immigrants are unskilled people eager to find jobs of any kind and prepared to accept difficult, unpleasant work at rates of pay that are low by American standards because these jobs are much better than whatever work (if any) they can find in their native land. (Carens, 1988: 210)

We noted in Chapter 4 the argument that jobs of the kind filled by migrant labour in the States offer terms and conditions which fail to live up to the promise of full participation in the accepted standards of life for US citizens; they do not rival even the precarious existence available outside employment, and can be filled only by workers with origins outside that 'community' of expectations. Illegal immigrants are particularly vulnerable in this respect, and Carens goes on to argue that: 'The existence of such a vulnerable, exploited underclass is incompatible with the goal of creating a society in which all members are regarded as having "equal social worth" and equal social, legal and political rights' (1988: 20).

We have here yet another use of the term 'underclass'; a reference to a disadvantaged group of workers with limited claims to the resources and protections of the society which appropriates their labour. Carens's deliberations weigh a liberal view rooted in the assumption of moral equality of all human beings against a utilitarian approach which takes into account the negative effects of immigration on the welfare state. The justice of the latter position must rest upon the requirement that only full members of a community (some would say contributors) have any legitimate call upon its resources, or as Carens puts it, that 'communities should look after their own' – and only their own.

Such arguments have even been applied to regional differences within the nation state, as we saw in the case of migration between states in the US. One issue for Carens is whether regional or national differences in welfare provisions reflect different choices or different capacities. Where they stem from initial inequality then the protection of certain provisions by the exclusion of outsiders is deemed morally unjustifiable. We can add to this that where the supposed outsiders have in fact been recruited to perform the least rewarding and most poorly paid tasks by another society their exclusion from the full rights of membership in that 'community' is even less justifiable. The situation is further compounded if the 'outsiders' are perceived to be in some other sense foreign: to be of distinct racial or ethnic origin. The receiving 'communities' may then object to their presence in defence of their common identity and distinctive way of life.

Marshall's treatment of citizenship has been argued by various writers (Yuval-Davis, 1990; Held, 1989) to be deficient in a number of ways, notably in its emphasis on social class as the main social differentiator, and its implicit confinement to the nation state. The issue of community membership needs to be brought to the forefront, raising questions which Marshall fails to address. Held argues:

> While it is the case that national sovereignty has been most often the victor when put to the test, the tension between

citizenship, national sovereignty and international law is marked, and it is by no means clear how it will be resolved.

Traditional concepts are argued to be undermined by 'the dynamics of a world economy which produces instabilities and difficulties within states and between states and which outreach the control of any single "centre"'.

The construction of a labour supply with a particular, inferior, relation to the nation state and therefore with limited claims to membership of the 'community' which that state represents is one instance of this dynamic. It poses a knot of problems for the relationship between the construction of an 'underclass', the status of outsider, and claims to social rights, which welfare provisions are inadequate to solve. In fact, access to welfare is one of the central issues in the denial of full membership to the migrant worker and there have been a number of different ways of restricting this access.

US LABOUR RESERVOIRS

Perhaps the best known example of an 'outlaw' status for migrant workers is the Hispanic 'wetback' population who gain illegal entry to the US across its border with Mexico. Mexican workers, both legal and illegal, together with others from the Caribbean basin, form the core of the contemporary pattern of migration, and have already been mentioned in the context of social exclusion and inferior conditions of employment. They are typically found in industries with high seasonal variation and with high vulnerability to unemployment. Migration from Mexico became established at the beginning of this century when the expansion of US agriculture in the South-west dealt with labour shortages by recruiting cheap Mexican labour. The establishment of a border control in 1924 marked an attempt to control the ebb and flow of such labour, defining it as illegal, and there were large scale deportations in the depression years. Migration built up again in the 1940s and Mexico entered into the Bracero agreement in 1942 to formalise American use of migrant labour.

This group of workers stood in many ways outside the indigenous social structure. They undermined the power of trade unions to negotiate acceptable pay and conditions, and were argued to be displacing local workers who would not accept the low wages offered. The Bracero programme expanded well into the 1950s, and from the 1960s onwards a land crisis in Mexico and a fall in agricultural production fuelled continuing internal and international migration. Unemployment in the northern cities of Mexico was as high as 30–40 per cent in the 1970s, and wages were roughly one-third of the US legal minimum. Border control and the prevention of illegal entry have now become major political concerns; Cohen suggests that official figures account for only about one-third of all migrants (1987: 57), and whilst such estimates may be contested there is no doubt about the substantial scale of unrecorded migration; in 1984 there were over 1 million apprehensions of illegal aliens, 94 per cent of them Mexicans.

In the 1970s illegal migration came to be construed as 'a severe national crisis' (Cohen, 1991: 60), and popular perceptions are not far removed from the Victorian image of a social residuum:

> Numbers are exaggerated and negative individual characteristics are attributed to all migrants. Migrants are supposed to exhibit criminal traits, evade taxes, yet make exorbitant claims on welfare, medical services and housing, provide a cultural threat to mainstream North American values and deprive US workers of jobs that are rightfully theirs.

Predictably there is opposition to both legal and illegal migration on the grounds that this takes the country's jobs and resources, though this account has been challenged. Simon (1989), for example, argues that immigrants are typically young adults at the beginning of working life, and not likely to be a great drain on health resources. Their dependants (if any) do not usually come with them to the US and they are arguably net contributors to the country's resources.

Simon (1989: 289) presents data to show that migrants use fewer public services than do natives, whilst paying easily their fair share of taxes. Illegal immigrants in particular are unlikely to make any claim on public services, because of their precarious status, but are often paying both income tax and a social security contribution. This is not, however, the popular perception, though the other common argument against migration is job displacement. This view assumes a static number of jobs in the labour market, and sees the presence of migrant workers as depriving some native citizens of employment. Simon, however, argues that the jobs would remain unfilled without the migrants because of the low pay and poor conditions they offer, and in the absence of migrants would probably disappear as employers would not be prepared to raise the wage.

There are two key points of interest in relation to the wider debate about the nature and existence of an underclass: the popular construction of illegal migrants as an outsider group placing a strain on national resources, and the effect of their presence on the market for indigenous labour. The trade union view, of course, is that employment of migrants, and especially illegal migrants, distorts the labour market and makes it impossible to impose decent minimum requirements on employers. There has thus been created an 'underclass' in the sense of a reserve army of labour available for work which does not meet a standard acceptable to secure residents and full citizens of the US The presence of this population offers support to the view that there are jobs available for those willing to work, and that welfare dependants constitute an 'underclass' in another sense; optional withdrawal from the labour market.

THE CASE OF POSTWAR EUROPE

Migration is clearly an important dimension of the underclass debate, by virtue of the material circumstances of the migrants, popular perceptions of the threat they pose to national resources and culture, and the effect of their availability on the structure of the labour market. There is now an established literature on the disadvantaged position of migrant workers in both Britain and America, and on corresponding social divisions in production and consumption (see for example Cross, 1992). The framework for what follows here differs from that of preceding chapters and breaks with the British/American comparison by focusing on a specific contemporary issue: migration within and into the European Community.

If we take seriously Yuval-Davis's reference to the construction of the collectivity, then free labour movement in Europe, given the very varied history of migration into member states, poses some intriguing problems. My conceptual and substantive focus is broadened here to consider issues of social inclusion in the context of a European labour market, and the use and abuse of 'outsiders'. 'In several industrialised states of Western Europe foreign citizens make up 10 to 15 per cent of the labour force' (Hammar, 1990: 1). The use of migrant labour is by no means confined to those countries included in membership of the European Community (EC), though questions have recently arisen concerning labour flows into and within the EC. The creation of the European Community effectively established a virtually free labour market for the original six, and currently twelve, member states. In the early years Italy was the only one of the EC countries with a labour surplus, and movement across borders within the EC was small. Although the expansion of EC membership and the changing labour market conditions of the 1970s and 1980s have meant some change in the relationship between the member states, debate about labour flows have mostly concerned movement into the EC from outside.

European countries have adopted different means of controlling their migrant labour, some of which are reviewed below, but the broad picture is the same for all: populations of workers have been created to occupy an extremely vulnerable labour market position, often with very limited rights in their country of employment. R. Moore (1977) identifies three categories of migrant worker: foreign workers (i.e. non-EC nationals), ex-colonial workers, and illegal migrants. All of them, argues Cohen (1987: 113), 'characteristically enjoy less favourable civil, legal and political status. Their family life is limited or prohibited, their housing is inferior, their rights as employees are often markedly worse than indigenous workers, while in most European countries they are disenfranchised and unorganised in trade unions.'

These workers are typically seen as part of a reserve army of labour (Castles and Kosack, 1985) through which the indus-trialised countries of Europe exploit the cheap, mobile and disposable labour of migrants from the Third World or southern and, increasingly, eastern Europe. Their exclusion from full social (and often legal) citizenship raises questions with implications for our understanding and conceptualisation of the 'underclass'.

Migrant workers are mainly to be found in the highly industrial-ised countries of northern Europe, estimated to contain almost 10 million migrants, or nine-tenths of the West European total (Castles and Kosack, 1985: 3). The majority arrived in the late 1950s and early 1960s, migrating from underdeveloped countries suffering high levels of unemployment or underemployment. Like Hispanic workers in the US, they are employed because they are willing to work on terms unacceptable to indigenous labour; commonly lacking citizenship rights they have an immediate disadvantage, intended to be easily expendable. Castles (1984) has provided an account of early postwar migration, and the main features of the labour flows he documents are summarised below.

Postwar Britain, France and the Netherlands were able to draw substantially on their colonial and ex-colonial populations as a source of cheap labour. For Britain the major sources were the Republic of Ireland and the Commonwealth, though the European Voluntary Worker scheme (Kay and Miles, 1992) recruited workers on restricted permits of various kinds to fill temporary labour demand created by the postwar boom. The slightly later flow of New Commonwealth workers throughout the 1950s was subject (at first) to no conditions or formal constraints; as British or Commonwealth citizens they had the right of free entry, until controls were introduced in the 1960s and thereafter, in response to racial tension. Since the 1970s there have also been workers coming from the Philippines, North Africa and Latin America.

In France, citizens from the colonies and former colonies were, as with Britain, able to enter freely and there was migration from North and West Africa. In addition, recruiting arrangements were established with South European countries, though clandestine labour came to dominate, rising from 26 per cent in 1948 to 82 per cent by 1968 (Castles, 1984). By 1970 there were 3 million foreign migrants in France, 1 million of them non-European; an under-estimate, as French nationals from the colonies are not classified as foreign. As with other countries there was a gradual shift in balance towards Third World migration throughout the 1970s, with the Third World share of the migrant population rising to almost half by 1981.

Early postwar migration to the Netherlands was also from former colonial links, with workers usually arriving as full citizens. The need for active recruitment from elsewhere really only became established after 1965 when migration was encouraged from southern Europe, though numbers were cut in times of unemployment. Again there was a shift towards the use of Third World labour throughout the 1970s, and this accounted for almost one-third of foreign labour by 1981. Colonial workers had full rights, whilst south Europeans were viewed as temporary residents.

In contrast to these three countries, West Germany, Switzerland and Belgium have relied principally on a guest worker system of labour migration. In Germany the Bundesansalt für Arbeit (BfA) was set up to recruit workers initially for agriculture but soon also for industry. The first agreement was with Italy in 1955 and then Greece, Turkey, Morocco, Portugal, Tunisia and Yugoslavia followed. During the 1960s Turkish workers came to predominate, making up 40 per cent of all foreign migrants. The workers were to be recruited and disposed of as labour demand dictated on a strict guest worker basis which allowed for the export of unemployment, though towards the end of the 1970s the presence of Third World migrants of refugee status also increased.

Switzerland followed a strong policy of large scale import of labour between 1945 and 1974 on a much more rigidly controlled guest worker system. By 1973 fully one-third of the labour force was made up of foreign workers. By far the largest proportion have always been the Italians, though with some workers from the neighbouring countries of Germany, Austria and France. The share of this latter group has declined since 1960 while the presence of workers from southern Europe (Spain, Turkey and Yugoslavia) increased. There have also been refugees from Latin America and Eastern Europe.

In Belgium, after the Second World War, there was a formally organised system of recruitment from southern European countries, mainly Italy, to work in Belgian heavy industry. This system was abolished in 1963 but the flow of workers continued, often entering on tourist visas, with Spanish, Moroccan and Turkish workers increasingly among the migrants. In 1974 all but EC workers were banned from entry, though clandestine immigration continued. The entry of workers has since been held at a minimum, though with a shift towards a Third World presence; as Spanish and Italian workers have left, Turks and Moroccans have arrived.

CONTROL OF SUPPLY

So the developed nations of northern Europe have, by a number of means, drawn on reserves of labour from outside their boundaries. Each has endeavoured, in a different way, to define the terms and conditions of their presence. Accordingly the rights and status of foreign workers show considerable variation between countries, and are directly related to the differing style and intensity of attempts to control their presence. By the early 1970s almost all of the countries discussed above faced the problem of control, and began to seek ways of limiting or dismissing their foreign workers, often urged on by social and political movements based on racist sentiments. A number of ways of doing so were introduced, some of which were inherent in the original terms under which migrants were allowed into the country concerned.

The common popular assumption in Britain was that black workers from the New Commonwealth countries had come for only a temporary period. Urban unrest and the obvious expansion of the black population prompted controls in the 1960s, the first of which required that Commonwealth migrants must obtain a voucher of employment before they would be granted entry (1962). Subsequent Acts of 1968 and 1971 placed restrictions on British passport holders in the Commonwealth, and workers who had planned a temporary stay were thus nudged into more permanent settlement. A further limiting factor came with the 1981 Nationality Act, which tightened up the rules under which full citizenship was available and placed increasing control on the entry of dependants.

In France too there was a crisis over immigrant workers in the early 1970s. In September 1973 a ban was placed on further immigration, and in 1979 a payment of £1,000 was authorised for unemployed migrants prepared to return home. Further restrictions were introduced in 1980 through legislation which combined work and residence permits and which in effect enabled the French to export unemployment. An amnesty was offered for illegal immigrants in 1981, though only half of the estimated 300,000 came forward. Many employers were not, however, prepared to offer regular employment and there were subsequent deportations. Much of the related political debate is cast in terms of the 'identity of our national community' (Silverman, 1992: 142).

The Netherlands shows a set of responses similar to the French, though with a different long term emphasis. As with France there are two categories of migrants, those from the ex-colonies and later migrants from Mediterranean countries. The latter group in particular was regarded as temporary labour, and the attempt was made to use them as a means of responding to economic fluctuations, where necessary exporting unemployment to their country of origin. In 1974 migration was called to a halt, and restrictive policies were put in place. Border controls were tightened and illegal immigrants deported, whilst the rights of migrants to unemployment benefit were cut.

West Germany attempted to build in control from the start, with migrant workers seen as temporary and expendable labour to be taken up or disposed of according to market requirements. These workers had only limited rights of residence associated with the need for their labour, though demand was such that in the early stages some migrants were encouraged to settle. A sudden ban on immigrant labour in 1973, a precedent for similar moves in a number of other countries, represented an attempt to reduce foreign labour. Some workers left because of the withdrawal of permits, after which they lost their residence rights. Others left because of unemployment or falling earnings. By the late 1970s the number of foreign migrants began to rise again, but increasingly through the arrival of dependants, a sign of long term settlement. A good proportion of the foreign population, however, have residence permits which allow deportation in a wide variety of circumstances, and they are denied a wide range of civil rights.

Switzerland has employed the strictest control of migrant workers, and is arguably the country most dependent on this source of labour. Seasonal workers spend only part of the year in the country, while frontier workers enter across the border each day to work. This is an extreme case of the use of foreign labour and the denial of full membership of the community. As in other countries there were restrictions in the early 1970s, more easily enforced given the very temporary nature of most migrants' status. By the late 1970s there was a further increase, especially in the most precarious groups; the seasonal and frontier workers. Naturalisation policy is extremely restricted, with a 12-year residence requirement (difficult for seasonal workers) and many other demanding conditions.

In Belgium there was a ban on the immigration of non-EC foreigners from August 1974, though clandestine immigration continued for a few years after that. A number of the illegal migrants were deported in the late 1970s, and employers fined, and there has since been an extremely restrictive policy on the entry of foreign migrants. Although labour migration was curtailed in 1974 the inflow of dependants has continued and Belgium's policy on this matter is quite liberal. Dependants who enter Belgium in this way have little difficulty in obtaining work permits themselves. There has, however, been resistance from some local authorities who refuse to register immigrants as resident.

MIGRANTS IN THE SOCIAL STRUCTURE

In brief, countries with access to a colonial population could exploit this source of labour (Britain, France and Holland), while others relied on some form of guest worker system (Germany, Belgium and Switzerland):

> Jobs filled by these workers were ones which were less acceptable to the indigenous work force. Immigrants were disproportionately employed in jobs which required arduous physical effort, had poor working conditions, and offered little security, and in some instances their employment was subject to seasonal variation and redundancy. These features of the work experience were common to ex-colonial labour and guest workers alike (Nanton, 1991: 192).

Similarly Gordon (1989) argues that although there is considerable variety in the uses to which migrants' labour is put – growing low level service sector jobs, or jobs in a declining manufacturing sector – 'they are mostly destined for routine manual work at the bottom of the occupational hierarchy' (p. 17). The particular patterns of employment in different countries will reflect 'varying forms of discrimination and closure in the indigenous labour market', but to much the same end.

The common pattern is confinement to a narrow range of low status, insecure work, which would otherwise be difficult to fill, and which is often subject to fluctuations in demand. Almost all of the countries discussed above instituted a system of labour migration in the postwar period which was intended to be temporary, though countries differed in the nature and rigidity of the mechanisms established to permit control of the situation. Germany and Switzerland were more successful than the other countries in reducing their foreign workforce in the period after 1973 (Gordon, 1989: 22), although the concentration of migrants in particular sorts of work limits their disposability. So does the gradual shift in orientation which seems to have occurred for the migrants.

In the first phase of migration the interests of employer, governments and workers seemed reasonably consistent: the employers wanted a flexible source of cheap temporary labour, the migrants wanted to stay for a limited period to save sufficient funds to improve their situation at home. Despite their inferior position in the 'host' labour market they were nevertheless offered better opportunities and income than were available in their country of origin. The second phase of the migratory process was family unification. Initially this followed when workers found they were not making sufficient progress by virtue of their own employment, and dependants arrived *also as workers* to add to their efforts. As a second generation grew up in the new country the prospects of the migrants returning became increasingly remote. Although by this time the demand for labour in these countries had considerably diminished the migrants had come to fill a particular slot in the labour force, and were anyway not so easily removed as had been at first anticipated.

The general trend has been away from the guest worker pattern, which proved hard to sustain, and towards much more permanent settlement, though with migrants holding inferior formal and informal status in the majority of countries. Their rights are often restricted, especially politically, they can be threatened with deportation for transgression of their conditions of residence, and they occupy a distinctly inferior position in the social and occupational structure. Even where migrants have made the transition to citizenship, or in other cases arrived as citizens, this has not guaranteed full social inclusion. Allen and Macey (1990: 388) comment upon an increasingly common distinction between nationality as ascribed by birth, and citizenship which may be conferred; a distinction, they argue, which 'strikes at the very heart of the concept of citizenship as including civil, political and social rights embedded in institutions'.

There have been racist responses of some kind to the immigrant population in almost all of the countries mentioned above, and access to social resources remains limited. A second generation is now growing up for whom there is no place in the labour market but who have no real ties with their parents' country of origin. The need for labour reserves in the postwar labour boom, usually to fill the jobs rejected by the 'host' population, has created an 'underclass' of a particular kind, ethnically or racially distinct, in inferior employment and increasingly unemployment, and often denied both formal and social citizenship. A precarious claim on social resources or the need for employment as a condition of residence can force them into work which full citizens of the receiving country would probably reject. Even where migrants have gained full citizenship, discrimination severely limits their prospects.

There has of course been debate about the suitability of a terminology of exclusion for migrant labour, such as sub- or lumpenproletariat (Castles and Kosack, 1985), terms arguably equivalent to the notion of the 'underclass'. As part of the workforce can migrants correctly be termed an underclass? Migrant labour has clearly been used to perform a particular function in terms of the labour needs of industrialised economies which leaves the migrant in a precarious social and economic position, and all of the issues reviewed so far in connection with the underclass debate apply to them: labour market disadvantage, social exclusion, and stigmatisation. Their position inevitably raises questions about what constitutes membership of a social and economic 'community' and under what circumstances and by what mechanisms the rights to such membership can be denied. These questions are just now arising in a new context, in relation to what has been termed 'Fortress Europe'.

THE EMERGENCE OF A EUROPEAN PROBLEM

The circumstances discussed above combine to pose an interesting challenge to the concept of European citizenship and European integration. A hint of the nature of the problem is given by the extension of EC membership in southern Europe. Whilst the status of some migrants has been improved by the entry of their countries of origin into the EC it should be noted that there was some concern about the possibility of a large sweep of labour migration into the North with the membership of the Mediterranean countries of Greece, Spain and Portugal. In fact, it was stipulated that the free movement of labour from these countries would come into effect only after a transitional period. Yet these countries are themselves experiencing problems of illegal entry.

The right of free movement of labour raises interesting questions, given that migration into Europe from non-EC countries is much greater than movement between EC countries. The long term trend in migration has meant a shift in the balance between European and Third World migrants such that the latter group makes up over 40 per cent of the minority populations of Britain, France and Germany (Castles, 1984: 89).

The northern Member States realised too late that the workers they had imported from Turkey and North Africa in the sixties and early seventies did not come only to work and then allow themselves to be sent back home afterwards. They came as guest workers and became immigrants . . . the result is: vulnerable groups of immigrants, uncertain about their future, dreaming of returning to their country of origin but knowing that they and their children no longer have a future there. Often too, living with the bleak prospect of lack of work and in poverty. (Hoogenboom, 1992: 42)

By 1984 3.3 million migrants lived in the original six countries of the EC, making up 5.5 per cent of the total active labour market. Only one-fifth came from other EC6 countries, one-fifth came from the new members Greece, Spain or Portugal, one-fifth came from Turkey, and the remaining two-fifths came from other countries, notably Yugoslavia, non-EC European countries and North Africa. In other words, access to the EC labour market has been more important to those outside the EC than internal movement has been to those within it. These figures reflect some of the changes that have been under way since the restrictions of the mid-1970s (Baldwin-Edwards, 1991). One feature of the 1980s has been the unprecedented number of asylum seekers, who in 1985 exceeded foreign workers. Whilst they are commonly denied work permits they will inevitably join the ranks of clandestine labour. There has also been extensive reunification of the families of guest workers, marking their transition to permanent settlers; considerable illegal immigration into southern Europe, mainly from North Africa, which more than equals legal migration; a re-emergence of the guest worker system, for mainly skilled workers; and the beginning of a flow of migration from Eastern Europe: 4–8 million are anticipated over the next few years (*Migration News Sheet*, Brussels, February 1991). In Germany workers from the east have to a great extent displaced the Turkish labour force (Baldwin-Edwards, 1991), and similar patterns could emerge elsewhere in Europe.

A high level of illegal migration into southern Europe is largely the result of proximity to underdeveloped countries where demographic pressures are pushing people to seek access of some kind to the more developed economies of Europe; that is to those countries which since the 1970s have sought to limit entry. In the southern countries immigration control is much weaker and the coastal border vulnerable to illicit entry. There is also a large informal sector in the economies of the South which offers a range of opportunities to illegal entrants. Throughout the 1980s there have been various regularisation programmes with differing degrees of take-up in Spain, Italy and France. These have been introduced alongside penalties for both employers and workers who continue to operate illegally.

The shift towards Third World migration has accelerated to the extent that there are 13 million legally settled non-Europeans in the 12 countries of the EC (Nanton, 1991), and 15 million non-EC nationals (Allen and Macey, 1990: 378):

> An estimated 60 per cent of those settled in France and 70 per cent in Germany and the Netherlands are citizens of countries outside the EC. This foreign population comprises a predominance of North Africans in France, Turks in Germany, Turkish and Moroccan communities in the Netherlands, and Moroccans in Belgium. (Nanton, 1991: 191)

Generally speaking the policy is now one of stabilisation, which combines attempts to prevent further entry with an explicit policy of 'integration', but the differing circumstances and policies of EC member states on the issue of labour migration threatens to become a problem. Some curious anomalies are emerging as a result of the free movement of EC nationals. Allen and Macey (1990: 381) point out, for example, that people of the British Dependent Territory of Hong Kong are denied the right of abode in Britain while the residents of Macao, who have full Portuguese citizenship rights, have access to Britain as EC nationals. Much of the controversy concerns the position of non-EC nationals and there have been calls for the standardisation of policy on border control, alongside more limited agreements in inter-governmental groupings.

FREE MOVEMENT OF LABOUR

Despite the aim of the Single European Act of 1992 to establish free movement of goods and persons there has been no clear agreement on the rather ambiguous position of non-EC nationals seeking entry to one member state from another. Although the European Parliament has argued that this matter should fall under EC competence, a General Declaration appended to the Single

European Act reserves the right of governments to take whatever measures are appropriate with regard to external migration (Baldwin-Edwards, 1991: 207). One grouping of countries, the Schengen Group of Benelux, France and Germany, agreed in 1985 on the removal of internal border controls and the strengthening of external ones and have since extended their membership. Negotiation has thus occurred in a selected number of countries, without public debate and bypassing EC institutions. Developments of this kind are overt threats to the basis of European policy and practice, though there has more generally been agreement on the need to limit immigration. However:

> While there is a growing awareness that integrated measures are needed at Community level, the traditional view is that the treatment of aliens remains an area which belongs to state sovereignty. This view is apparently difficult to reconcile with the requirements of the internal market. (Hoogenboom, 1992: 36)

A major problem has been how far freedom of movement across borders within the EC should be extended to legally resident non-EC nationals. Potentially, the immigration decisions of one country could have an ultimate impact on those of another (as with the Portuguese/British example cited above). The member states differ in both the nature and structure of their economies, and in the nature of their policy and their degree of practical control over immigration. As we noted above, the countries of the South have higher levels of clandestine migration, and this has in part been dealt with by offers of regularisation. Are these regularised migrants then to be granted freedom of movement within Europe, and would selective restriction be consistent with the Community's aims of equal treatment and social justice, or the establishment of an internal market? Hoogenboom argues that restrictions not only deny the logic of the internal market but frustrate one of the primary objectives of Community law, which is to raise the general standard of living. The issue is one not simply of access to material resources, but of the systematic inequality suffered by non-EC and more specifically non-European ethnic groups. Who is to be included in the generalised raising of standards?

Hoogenboom (1992: 44) offers a guide to the powers of the community on this matter, as expressed in the Treaty governing free movement of persons:

The Treaty does not restrict free movement and equality of treatment to EC nationals. Article 3(c) expressly refers to the free movement of *persons*, without limiting it to EC nationals, and Article 7, which contains the prohibition on discrimination, and Article 48, which lays down the free movement of workers, do not reserve these norms for citizens who are nationals of one of the Member States.

The dependants of a community national who is employed in a Member State other than his/her own have full rights to join the worker and, if they wish, accept employment regardless of their own nationality. The question of whether these rights apply to the families of non-EC workers who are legally resident and employed within the EC is an important one with serious implications about the rights of settlement, though the Court of Justice has ruled against the application of Article 48 to non-EC nationals.

The richer Member States have resisted moves by the Commission to set out a procedure for consultation on immigration policies on the grounds that this impinges on sovereignty. The Court ruled that migration policies in respect of third states fell under social issues and included social integration with regard to employment and working conditions. The opposing countries argued that the Commission wished not only to arrange a procedure, but to lay down the aims and thus determine the outcome (Hoogenboom, 1992: 47). The Court's ruling here was that the Commission was not empowered to extend consultation in the areas it wished, or to make the securing of conformity an objective of consultation. A different Court decision ruled that the Commission is empowered to promote co-operation between Member States in respect of non-EC nationals, and opportunities for cross-border labour could be sought for certain categories (Hoogenboom 1992: 48). Hoogenboom also notes that some new provisions inserted into the EC Treaty give the Commission institutions at least some competence in the field of free movement of non-EC nationals.

The concern over sovereignty in the above conflict is readily apparent in an annexe to the Single European Act which asserts the right of Member States to take the measures they deem necessary for the control of migration (Hoogenboom 1992: 49). The Act also contains, however, a declaration of co-operation without prejudice to the powers of the Community with regard to the entry, movement and residence of nationals of third countries:

> Taking both of these declarations together, it can be deduced that on the one hand the Member States wish to retain their power to control immigration into their territories, but that on the other they acknowledge the powers of the Community in the fields of entry, movement and residence of non-EC nationals concerning the crossing of the internal borders. (Hoogenboom 1992: 50)

Member States who wish to do so, however, can sidestep the whole issue by granting nationality and thus conferring the rights of free movement of the EC national. This, of course, is why there is some concern to achieve standardised policy with regard to migration, despite the spirit of the Social Charter: 'The Charter is no more than a statement of intent. . . . Still for Europe's immigrants the document does at least offer official recognition of their right to freedom of movement and association' (Ireland, 1991: 463).

The issue, however, remains that under the banner of defence of sovereignty many of the more prosperous countries of Europe wish to defend their borders and their resources from the presence and claims of 'outsiders'. Collaboration on the basis of a European Community has so far come into conflict with the right to decide on membership of and access to the national 'community'. A final agreement on free movement for non-EC nationals would mean that the greater accessibility of south European countries to Third World migrants, and particularly the regularisation of clandestine labour, would ultimately affect the populations and resources of the more developed (and richer) countries of the North. One of the fears which underlies resistance to this situation is that it opens up the possibility of 'social dumping'. Free movement of labour in an integrated market would mean that states with high unemployment or low social welfare provision could effectively export their unemployment to states with jobs to offer or with better welfare provisions.

One way to prevent this would be to establish a social dimension to the single market, of the kind represented by the Charter of Social Rights, which is not at present legally binding. By standardising terms and conditions of employment, minimum wages, equal treatment by gender and race, social security systems and rights, etc., national barriers to labour mobility could be removed without the fear of social dumping (Roche, 1992: 215). But this would also limit the degree of exploitation of foreign labour in a way which would not suit employers, and would confer full social citizenship upon the migrants, something which has so far been resisted. This is one of the reasons for the desire for strict and standardised policy on immigration, but should this be achieved there will still be a reluctance on the part of some countries to accept the consequences of the previous immigration policy of others – a resistance to conferring social citizenship upon migrants whom they would never have allowed across their borders. These questions are all the more pressing given the break-up of the eastern bloc, and the emergence of new nations in the East, many of which see the solution to their problems as entry into Europe. If they are not received into the EC as nations, their populations will as individuals seek their own way in.

MIGRATION AND THE UNDERCLASS

This chapter has highlighted two related problems: the concern of more affluent nation states to protect their resources and culture from 'outsiders' who hope for access to their superior material standards; and the particular problems posed for these states should they wish, periodically, to appropriate the labour of these outsiders whilst continuing to deny them full inclusion. When a group of countries seeks to forge a new community of interests then the definition and defence of their internal and external borders will be an immediate issue, as we have seen in the case of the European Community. The desire for entry by 'outsiders', and their partial inclusion – sometimes by invitation and sometimes by stealth – has come to be seen as the creation of an 'underclass'.

Earlier chapters examined the variety of definitions and explanations of this term which dominate contemporary debate. The basic disagreements are between whether a structural or cultural explanation is most persuasive, and whether the concept refers only to unemployment and state dependence, or more broadly to labour market disadvantage. Whichever definition or explanation is adopted, the 'underclass' seems to stand as a counterpart to the idea of social citizenship: the guarantee of inclusion in the established and legitimate expectations of society. The position of migrant workers is interesting in a number of respects. Certainly if we define the underclass as benefit dependent then the least privileged of the migrants would be excluded – clandestine workers with no rights and legal migrants allowed residence only by virtue of employment.

A full understanding of migrant labour clearly rests upon an appreciation not only of civic status in relation to formal citizenship and social support, but also of their structural position in the labour market. It is by virtue of their vulnerability rather than their unemployment and state dependence that they might be included in the category of the underclass. Such a move would necessarily meet with objections on the grounds that those in employment cannot be assigned a position 'outside of class' (Morris and Irwin, 1992). And yet migrants are often involved in work which would (reasonably) be rejected by those with some claim to state support. These conceptual problems suggest an inadequacy in the notion of the underclass, but more generally reveal a problem in approaches to structured inequality.

Such inequality we have found to operate on two dimensions: that of civic status, and that of position in the labour market, as is especially apparent in the case of migrant labour. On the one hand are questions of formal citizenship, claims to state resources, social perceptions of the status of dependence, and the standards of living achievable by this means. On the other hand are rankings by skill, prospects of employment, vulnerability to unemployment, and the terms and conditions under which an individual worker can still be expected to labour. At the extreme position on both dimensions of inequality are the clandestine migrants, below even those conventionally termed the underclass.

Conclusion

This book began by observing that the two complementary social institutions of secure full time employment for men and the nuclear family household can no longer be taken for granted in British or American society. The high and enduring levels of male unemployment and the increasing proportion of single parent households have been linked together through the concept of the underclass, a term applied to a group portrayed as living outside society's norms and values, in a condition of dependence. This phenomenon poses problems of explanation and interpretation, as well as challenging established models for representing social structure. The creation of a residual category of the underclass, however, is a response which confines attention to a limited social grouping, allowing perceptions of the rest of society to remain largely undisturbed.

The history of social thought shows a number of equivalent notions in the past: the redundant population, the lumpenproletariat, and the social residuum, all constructed in terms of a basic immorality manifest variously in sexual abandon, criminality, vagrancy, the abhorrence of labour, and an inclination to dependency. It is this last tendency which has been the main focus for concern, both in Victorian England and in contemporary Britain and America. Dependency then, as now, is largely explained as a defect of character, though there is also a fear that adequate provision for the poor could undermine the work incentive among lower-paid workers. Even Marx, who saw poverty as an inevitable product of capitalism, with the poor as its helpless victims, identifies a depraved and decadent 'social scum'.

The relationship between this residuum and the rest of the labouring population has never been made entirely clear, though the assumption of a sharp division between the two seems largely uncontested. For Marx the lumpenproletariat was a category apart from the real proletariat, while Mayhew distinguished between the vagabonds and the citizens, and even Booth, who emphasised the poverty of the working population, had a category of 'loafers', 'incapable of improvement'. Indeed, the story of past and present welfare policy in both Britain and America rests upon the attempt to separate the worthy from the unworthy poor. Yet the very writers who affirmed the distinction also provided evidence which might call it into question.

The problem remains in contemporary debate, and not just in relation to the surveillance of benefit claimants and the preservation of the work incentive. A particular feature of economic change in the 1980s has been what Beck (1992) calls pluralised underemployment; the de-standardisation of employment patterns, alongside chronic insecurity. Like the 'underclass', the workers affected are also cut adrift from conventional class categories, but whether they belong with the long term unemployed, and those more definitively out of the workforce, is not clear. In the early writings of the nineteenth century it was personal morality that marked the division, and also explained it, though there was always a threat of the corruption and contamination of those above. A later individualised account of the residuum was rooted in eugenics, and the associated view that to solve the problem one simply eliminated the people, by stopping them from breeding.

Whilst eugenics has not been strongly espoused in contemporary approaches to the 'underclass', the idea of morality as the basis for non-employment and dependency is certainly apparent, and there have been renewed efforts to distinguish between the deserving and the undeserving. This distinction was arguably present in the British system of social security established after the war and to a considerable degree still in operation. The provision had been intended to establish a system of universal rights, and there was optimism that it would prove the means to establish social citizenship. One problem is that benefit has never been able to shake off the associations of the Poor Law, whereby receipt of Public Assistance shows moral failure. This has recently been exacerbated by assertions of a dependency culture, and a tightening up on the policing of benefit claimants.

Beveridge's proposal had been for a system of insurance against unemployment which would provide benefit indefinitely, as of right, based on the pooling of risk. This recommendation was never put into practice, and from the start insurance benefit was time limited. The long term unemployed have always had to resort to means tested benefit; the gradual erosion of the insurance based benefit has also meant that increasing numbers of the short term unemployed rely upon a means tested supplement. This involves tighter surveillance and greater personal shame and exposure. Marshall saw that one problem in the achievement of social citizenship might be that the economic equalisation offered by social security could be offset by the loss of status through the stigma attached to claiming. Arguably this is what has happened, heightened by the lengthening duration of unemployment, the doubtful adequacy of the benefit and the tightening of conditions of eligibility. There are also indications that social judgement and moral condemnation permeate the whole system for the administration of benefits.

In the British system social citizenship was never fully achieved, and claimants have never been entirely free from moral condemnation and therefore social exclusion. The notion of the underclass, defined in terms of state dependence, also carries this sense of moral judgement, although as we saw in chapter 4 there are competing usages. As I suggested in the Introduction, social citizenship and the underclass can be seen as linked concepts, the one suggesting social inclusion in both moral and material terms, and the other certainly indicating material and economic exclusion, but often also linked to moral failure. There may, of course, be conditions attached to social rights and social inclusion. Thus, underlying the guarantees made by the British social security system is the condition of 'actively seeking work', a condition which has received increasing emphasis in recent years. In the American system this conditional approach has been much more fully developed.

Though the early forms of welfare in the US differed little from those in Britain, a difference of emphasis did eventually emerge. The introduction of an insurance system came much later, and there was resistance to the idea of federal provision for the uninsured unemployed. Thus Hoover argued that state support in Europe had been a major contributor to the problem of unemployment there. Even under F.D. Roosevelt the emergency relief of the 1930s was fairly quickly curtailed, in part for fear of the destructive effects of dependence. The system of support that did develop distinguished much more sharply than the British system between social security and welfare, with the major welfare provision taking the form of assistance for widows through AFDC.

It is the explosion of access to AFDC, initially as a result of welfare rights campaigns, which lies behind the debate on the dependent 'underclass'. The work of Charles Murray has done much to popularise this term and he argues that the liberalisation of thinking about welfare in the 1960s and 1970s caused considerable damage. It is his contention that the idea of the disadvantaged as passive victims of forces beyond their control has eroded the view of self-sufficiency as an obligation of the individual and a source of personal pride. AFDC is seen to be implicated in this process by undermining family values and the work ethic and fostering a sub-culture of dependency. Poor socialisation then becomes the key issue in explanation. There is also an element of the rational choice perspective in his argument, which suggests that in financial terms it has become more attractive for a woman to claim AFDC as a sole parent, whilst living with her male partner, than for one or both of them to take low-paying work. This situation is argued to have been brought about by the loosening of conditions for claimants.

The phenomenon Murray describes is certainly disturbing, and also threatening: that of a young black population concentrated in the inner cities yet having no vested interest in a society from whose rewards they seem to be excluded. The criticisms of his position predictably concern his neglect of structural features of labour market change, and the resultant vulnerability of the young black population to unemployment. The fact that young black males do not have direct access to welfare benefits also weakens Murray's argument about a sub-culture of dependence. At the centre of his work, however, is a question of a different order, and one which has been present throughout the history of social policy in both Britain and America. How much responsibility should be collectively assumed by society for its most vulnerable members?

The idea of social citizenship has always been based both on rights and obligations, though the emphasis in social policy has usually been on the former. In the US there is now increasing stress placed on the obligations of citizenship, which are argued to be as much a part of social inclusion as rights. Eligibility for welfare is seen as the major vehicle by which social obligations could be enforced, though this clearly could be effective only for potential recipients. Many non-employed black youth are not directly eligible for welfare and hence not open to control of this kind. Quite apart from this practical issue, there is also the ethical question of whether social provision should be used as a tool of coercion, which partly depends upon the nature of the conditions likely to be imposed. Where the effect is to push claimants into low-paid, menial employment then there may be some encroachment upon the right to demand reasonable terms and conditions of work. Such jobs in the States have commonly been filled by illegal migrants, who have little choice but to accept them; as 'outsiders' they have no claim on the legal protections or welfare system which the country offers its own citizens. Should those citizens be reduced to this level?

Implicitly these problems raise questions about the structuring of the labour market, and the process by which particular groups are designated particular positions. This constitutes the major focus of a structural approach to understanding the 'underclass'; an approach which stands in opposition to either the sub-cultural or rational choice type of explanation. We saw that in the American literature there is some debate about whether race or class is the principal factor in the structural dynamic. The wish to emphasise race is largely in assertion of the fact that prejudice and discrimination continue to exist at all levels of American society, whilst the emphasis on class stems from awareness of considerable black social mobility since the 1960s. Whichever position is taken, the high incidence of black unemployment is explained by vulnerability, not poor socialisation, and this in turn is argued to explain high levels of black single parenthood.

The latter argument has been contested by those who point out that the decline of marriage is a characteristic of the general population, not just the lowest social stratum. Though this may be true, it is the very young age of some of the 'underclass' single parents which gives cause for concern. It remains possible, however, that this is a specific aspect of a broader phenomenon which reflects the declining viability of marriage. The same point has been made of the British data on single parenthood, though the situation in Britain is rather different. Certainly there is more welfare support for unemployed men, so that a connection between single parenthood, male unemployment and welfare incentives is harder to make. Furthermore, the fact that a majority of single parents in Britain eventually marry makes it difficult to construct an account based on a distinctive sub-culture of the underclass.

British concern has focused much more upon the position of the long term unemployed, and the concentration of unemployment in households than upon the position of single parents, and a problem arises here as to whether the individual or the household is the appropriate unit of analysis. The most explicit connection with the underclass debate has been anxiety about the emergence of a dependency culture, though there is a related concern about the work incentive, and suspicions of fraud and abuse. A more strictly academic interest has been how the concept of the underclass connects with theories of social stratification, or more specifically, how unemployment can be integrated into production-based accounts of social structure. Here we find the recurrence of a problem noted at the start of this Conclusion: the nature of the distinction between the unemployed and the underemployed.

Both groups are clearly disadvantaged, but to differing degrees, and there is probably some movement either way across the boundary between them. The existence of an underemployed group, which seems likely to have grown given the changing patterns of employment throughout the 1980s, calls attention away from non-employment and towards the structure and operations of the labour market. The 'underclass' of the non-employed and state dependent then appears as an extreme position in the broader context through which the sale of labour is negotiated and renegotiated. One factor in this process is the nature of provision by the state for those without work, and the level of support available has some impact on the lower level of wages that employers can expect workers to accept.

So, for example, the structure and operation of the labour market has a bearing on the position of single mothers who, in the US, are required to participate in Workfare if they are to receive benefit. The hope is that by enforced contact with the world of employment the women will eventually be able to leave the welfare roll. Commonly, however, they are unable to command a wage sufficient to free them from dependence on benefit because of the very poor quality of jobs available to them. The same is largely true in Britain both for single parents and for the wives of unemployed men. An emphasis on paid employment for single mothers, whilst in line with the increased presence of married women in the labour force, is in conflict with an emphasis on the mothering role. One explanation of the underclass has argued that the poor socialisation provided in single mother households is largely responsible.

The other gendered aspect of the underclass to emerge from the literature concerns the feminisation of poverty. The core of the argument is that society has pushed the burden of poverty on to a vulnerable population of lone mothers, who generally suffer higher (and rising) rates of poverty than the rest of the population. The alternative position is to blame the irresponsible behaviour of the women themselves, and also the nature of the welfare provision available to them, which is seen by some as an incentive to embark on motherhood. If they cannot be deterred from this path they can at least be subject to certain conditions attaching to receipt of welfare.

Women's position in the household, especially the situation of single mothers, raises a number of problems for conceptions of social inclusion. As welfare dependants they become stigmatised members of the underclass, failing in their role of socialisation. The gendered nature of the labour market means they are for the most part unable to earn sufficient to be self-supporting, and full time employment would in any case conflict with their mothering role. It is hard to see what full social inclusion would look like for these women, and without some reassessment of the sexual division of labour in society this will continue to be the case.

The other way in which the idea of social citizenship was argued to be inadequate was in the identification of the social community to which it applies, and the processes of exclusion, or only partial inclusion, which serve to defend it. An obvious example that has some bearing on the underclass debate is migration, particularly illegal migration, from Mexico and the Caribbean basin into the US. The migrants are denied normal citizenship rights, and used to fill jobs which would be unacceptable to full citizens. In this they themselves form an underclass, though their presence supports the argument that jobs are available for the 'indigenous' underclass, if only they would take them.

Much the same issues are apparent in the history of migration into Europe, and in the postwar period the more developed countries drew upon either colonial labour or guest workers with limited rights to fill their least desirable employment. If we take a view of the underclass which covers all those excluded from reasonable standards of employment, as in Wilson's early definition

(1978), then low level migrant labour, especially illegal migrants, would certainly be included. An interesting question which has arisen in the context of the single European market is whether the free movement of labour is to apply to migrant workers with origins outside the EC. There is resistance to surrendering state sovereignty over the treatment of 'aliens', though the implications of the Single European Act seem to point in this direction: the immigration decisions of one country could ultimately affect the capacity of others to control entry. The debate about who has access to the EC, and under what terms and conditions, is an example of the social construction of 'community', and correspondingly of 'outsiders'.

A number of points which have emerged from this review lead to some consideration of the structure of the labour market, and in particular the position of certain underprivileged groups, be they migrant labourers, single mothers, or unskilled workers. One issue is that jobs are available, but offering standards which fall well below those reasonably expected by full social citizens. The uses of migrant labour both in America and Europe suggest that this is true to some degree. More generally there is the question of whether there is a minimum acceptable standard of pay and employment conditions. There is naturally some relationship between welfare and employment, if only through political awareness that the setting of rates may affect the supply of low-paid labour. There is, however, evidence available which shows that work is valued in and of itself and for many need be no more than adequate financially in order to be minimally acceptable.

The issue of employment viability leads us to a question which has been tangential to the underclass debate. Should the term apply to the underemployed, a category which includes part time, seasonal and chronically insecure workers? The consensus in the literature seems to be against this, defining the underclass as outside the system of production, and therefore also of social class. This view is contestable, since much unemployment is understandable only in relation to labour market processes, but the emphasis in the underclass debate has in fact been more concerned with what are essentially status differences. This is apparent in two ways: the significance of material resources in securing full social inclusion, and the social stigma associated with state dependence which comes close to the moral blame attached to the nineteenth-century residuum.

As a concept, then, the underclass is useful in capturing status exclusion, despite the unfortunate implication of moral blame, and for this reason has served as a powerful tool of political rhetoric for both left and right. It is less useful or convincing in explanatory terms, though we have noted two principal schools of thought. Individual and household-level decisions are clearly relevant in the portrayal of the options people perceive to be open to them, and how they order their preferences. The extent to which there is rational calculative action is certainly of interest, as are sub-cultural orientations. But above and beyond this level of analysis must stand the functioning of the labour market, both in terms of the sorts of jobs on offer, and to whom they are available.

It is helpful to include analysis which takes in much more than the position of the unemployed and/or state dependent, and considers the restructuring and distribution of different types of employment in terms of broad social groupings and household structures. It has been clear from the material in other parts of this book that there is at least some interaction here with the availability and nature of state support, though there is little rigorous and systematic research on this topic. Analysis of this kind, if accomplished alongside a consideration of the foundation and conditions of social inclusion, could do much to change the terms of debate from a focus on the residual category of the underclass to a reconsideration of how sociologists think about social structures.

References

Ainsworth, W.H. (1839) *Jack Sheppard*, London.

Allen, S. and Macey, M. (1990) 'Race and ethnicity in the European context', *British Journal of Sociology*, 41: 375–93.

Armstrong, C.W, (1931) *The Survival of the Unfittest* (1927), London; revised edn 1931.

Atkinson, A.B. and Micklewright, J. (1988) *Turning the Screw*, Discussion paper TIDI/121, Suntory-Toyota International Centre, London School of Economics.

Auletta, K. (1982) *The Underclass*, New York: Random House.

Baldwin-Edwards, M. (1991) 'Migration after 1992', *Policy and Politics*, 19: 199–211.

Bane, M.J. (1988) 'Politics and policies of the feminization of poverty', in M. Weir, A.S. Orloff and T. Skocpol (eds) *The Politics of Social Policy in the United States*, Princeton, NJ: Princeton University Press, 381–96.

Banfield, E. (1968) *The Unheavenly City*, Boston: Little Brown.

Barbalet, J.M. (1988) *Citizenship*, Milton Keynes: Open University Press.

Beck, U. (1992) *The Risk Society*, London: Sage.

Bell, C. and McKee, L. (1985) 'Marital and family relations in times of male unemployment', in B. Roberts, R. Finnegan and D. Gallie (eds), *New Approaches to Economic Life*, Manchester: Manchester University Press.

Berger, P. and Berger, B. (1983) *The War Over the Family*, London: Hutchinson.

Beveridge, W. (1906) 'The problem of the unemployed', *Sociological Papers*, 3.

—— (1942) *Report on the Social Insurance and Allied Services*, Cmnd 6404, London: HMSO.

Blacker, C.P. (1926) *Birth Control and the State*, London: Kegan Paul.

—— (1937) *A Social Problem Group?*, Oxford: Oxford University Press.

Blanesburgh Report (1927) *Report of the Unemployment Insurance Committee*, 2 vols, London: HMSO.

Booth, C. (1902) *Life and Labour of the People of London*, London: Macmillan.

Bovenkerk, F. (1984) 'The Rehabilitation of the Rabble', *Netherlands Journal of Sociology*, 20: 13–42.

Boyer, P. (1978) *Urban Masses and Moral Order in America, 1820–1920*, Cambridge, Mass.: Harvard University Press.

Bradley, H. (1989) *Men's Work Women's Work*, Cambridge: Polity Press.

Bradshaw, J. and Morgan, J. (1987) *Budgeting on Benefit*, Occasional Paper No. 5, London: Family Policy Studies Centre.

Brown, J. (1989) *Why Don't They Go To Work?*, London: HMSO.

—— (1990) 'The focus on single mothers', in Murray (1990).

Buck, N. (1992) 'Labour market inactivity and polarisation', in D.J. Smith (ed.), *Understanding the Underclass*, London: Policy Studies Institute.

Burroughs, C. (1834) 'A discourse delivered in the chapel of the new poorhouse in Portsmouth, 1834', reprinted in D.J. Rothman (ed.), *The Jacksonians on the Poor*, New York: Arno Press, 1971.

Bussard, R. (1987) 'The "Dangerous Class" of Marx and Engels', *History of European Ideas*, 8: 675–92.

Carens, J.H. (1988) 'Immigration and the welfare state', in A. Gutman (ed.) *Democracy and the Welfare State*, Princeton, NJ: Princeton University Press, 207–30.

Carlyle, T. (n.d.) *English and Other Critical Essays*, London: Everyman.

Castles, S. (1984) *Here For Good*, London: Pluto Press.

Castles, S. and Kosack, G. (1985) *Immigrant Workers and Class Structure in Western Europe*, Oxford: Oxford University Press.

Cohen, R. (1987) *The New Helots*, Aldershot: Gower.

—— (1991) *Contested Domains*, London: Zed Books.

Congressional Budget Office (1987) *Work – Related Programs for Welfare Recipients*, Washington: CBO.

Cooke, D. (1989) *Investigating Tax and Supplementary Benefit Fraud*, London: Routledge.

—— (1992) 'Footnotes to the discussion', in Smith (1992), 55–8.

Cross, M. (ed.) (1992) *Ethnic Minorities and Industrial Change in Europe and North America*, Cambridge: Cambridge University Press.

Dahrendorf, R. (1985) Letter to *The Times*, 2 June.

Dahrendorf, R. (1992) 'Footnotes to the discussion' in D.J. Smith (1992).

Darwin, C. (1964) *On the Origin of Species* (1859), a facsimile of the first edition, Cambridge, Mass.: Harvard University Press.

—— (1871) *The Descent of Man*, London.

Davies, R.B., Elias, P. and Penn, R. (1991) *The Relationship Between a Husband's Unemployment and his Wife's Participation in the Labourforce*, mimeo, University of Lancaster.

Davies, C. and Ritchie, J. (1988) *Tipping the Balance*, London: DHSS/HMSO.

De Tocqueville, A. (1968) 'Memoir on pauperism', in S. Drescher, (ed.), *Tocqueville and Beaumont on Social Reform*, Cambridge, Mass.: Harvard University Press.

Deacon, A. (1976) *In Search of the Scrounger*, Occasional Papers on Social Administration, Leeds: Social Administration Research Trust.

—— (1982) 'An end to the means test? Social security and the Attlee government', *Journal of Social Policy*, 2: 288–306.

Deacon, A. and Bradshaw, J. (1983) *Reserved for the Poor*, Oxford: Basil Blackwell and Martin Robertson.

Department of Employment (1988) *Employment in the 1990s*, Cm 540, London: HMSO.

Dietz, M.G. (1987) 'Context is all: feminism and theories of citizenship', *Daedalus*, 116: 1–24.

Dilnot, A. and Kell, M. (1989) 'Men's unemployment and women's work', in A. Dilnot and P. Walker (eds), *The Economics of Social Security*, Oxford: Oxford University Press.

Dilnot, A. Kay, J. and Morris, C. (1984) *The Reform of Social Security*, Oxford: Institute of Fiscal Studies Oxford University Press.

Disraeli, B. (1845) *Sybil*, London.

Donzelot, J. (1979) *The Policing of Families*, London: Hutchinson.

Dugdale, R. (1877) *The Jukes*, New York: Putnam.

Ellwood, D. (1986) 'The spatial mismatch hyothesis', in R.B. Freeman and H.J. Holzer (eds), *The Black Youth Employment Crisis*, Chicago: Chicago University Press.

—— (1987) 'Valuing the US income support system for lone mothers', paper for the OECD Conference of National Experts on Lone Mothers, Paris.

Ellwood, D. and Bane, M.J. (1985) 'AFDC and family structure', in R.G. Ehrenberg (ed.), *Review of Labour Economics*, Vol. 7, Greenwich, Conn.: JAI Press.

—— and —— (1986) 'Slipping into and out of poverty', *Journal of Human Resources*, 21: 1–23.

Ellwood, D. and Summers, L. (1985) 'Poverty in America', Conference paper, Institute for Research on Poverty, University of Wisconsin, Madison.

Ermisch, J. (1986) *The Economics of the Family: Applications to Divorce and Remarriage*, Discussion Paper 140, London: CEPR.

Fainstein, N. (1987) 'The underclass mismatch hypothesis as an explanation for black economic deprivation', *Politics and Society*, 15: 403–51.

—— (1992) 'Race, class and segregation', paper presented at ISA conference, Committee 21, University of California, Los Angeles.

Fainstein, S., Gordon, I. and Harloe, M. (1992) *Divided Cities*, Oxford: Basil Blackwell.

Field, F. (1989) *Losing Out*, Oxford: Basil Blackwell.

Fraser, D. (1986) *The Evolution of the British Welfare State*, London: Macmillan.

Fullinwider, R.K. (1988) 'Citizenship and welfare', in A. Gutmann (ed.), *Democracy and the Welfare State*, Princeton, NJ: Princeton University Press, 261–78.

Gallie, D. (1988) 'Employment, unemployment and social stratification', in *Employment in Britain*, Oxford: Basil Blackwell, 465–92.

Gans, H.J. (1990) 'Deconstructing the underclass', *Journal of the American Planning Association*, 56: 271–7.

General Household Survey, London: HMSO.

Gershuny, J.I. (1979) 'The informal economy: its role in post-industrial society', *Futures*, 12: 3–15.

Giddens, A. (1973) *The Class Structure of the Advanced Societies*, London: Hutchinson.

Gilbert, B.B. (1966) *Evolution of National Insurance in Great Britain*, London: Michael Joseph.

Gilder, G. (1986) *Men and Marriage*, Gretna, Louisiana: Pelican.
—— (1987) 'The collapse of the American family', *The Public Interest*, 89: 20–5.
Gilroy, P. (1989) *There ain't no Black in the Union Jack*, London: Routledge.
Golding, P. and Middleton, S. (1982) *Images of Welfare*, Oxford: Martin Robertson.
Gordon, I. (1989) 'The role of international migration in the changing European labour market', in I. Gordon and A.P. Thirwall (eds), *European Factor Mobility*, London: Macmillan, 13–29.
Graham, H. (1987) 'Being poor: perceptions of coping strategies of lone mothers', in J. Brannen and G. Wilson (eds), *Give and Take in Families*, London: Allen & Unwin, 56–74.
Green, G. and Welniak, E. (1982) *Changing Family Composition and Income Differentials*, Washington DC: Government Printing Office.
Greenstein, R. (1985) 'Losing faith in losing ground', *New Republic*, 25 March.
Greenwood, J. (1976) 'A night in a work house' (1866), in Keating (1976), 33–53.
Gueron, J. (1988) 'State welfare employment initiatives', *Focus*, Spring: 17–24.
—— (1989) 'Work for people on welfare', *Public Welfare*, Winter: 7–12 and 48.
Hammar, T. (1990) *Democracy and the Nation State*, Aldershot: Avebury.
Harrington, M. (1984) *The New American Poverty*, New York: Holt, Rinehart & Winston.
Heath, A. (1992) 'The attitudes of the underclass', in Smith (1992).
Held, D. (1989) 'Citizenship and autonomy', in D. Held and J.B. Thompson (eds), *Social Theory of Modern Societies*, Cambridge: Cambridge University Press, 162–84.
Hill, M. (1974) *Policies for the Unemployed*, Poverty Pamphlet 15, London: Child Poverty Action Group.
Himmelfarb, G. (1984) *The Idea of Poverty*, London: Faber & Faber.
Hirschman, A.O. (1991) *The Rhetoric of Reaction*, Cambridge, Mass.: Harvard University Press.
Hogan, D.P. (1983) 'Structural and normative factors in single parenthood among black adolescents', paper presented at ASA annual conference, San Antonio.
Hogan, D.P. and Kitagawa, E.M. (1985) 'The impact of social status, family structure and neighborhood on the fertility of black adolescents', *American Journal of Sociology*, 90: 825–55.
Hoogenboom, T. (1992) 'Integration into society and free movement of non-EC nationals', *European Journal of International Law*, 3: 36–52.
Howe, L. (1985) 'The deserving and the undeserving', *Journal of Social Policy*, 14: 49–72.
Hunter, R. (1965) *Poverty* (1904), New York: Harper & Row.
Ireland, P.R. (1991) 'Facing the true "Fortress Europe": immigrants and politics in the EC', *Journal of Common Market Studies*, 5: 457–80.

Irwin, S. and Morris, L.D. (1993) 'Social security or economic insecurity?', *Journal of Social Policy*.

Jencks, C. (1985) 'How poor are the poor?', *New York Review*, 32.

—— (1992) *Rethinking Social Policy*, Cambridge, Mass.: Harvard University Press.

Jones, C. (1934) *Social Survey of Merseyside*, Liverpool: Liverpool University Press.

Jones, G. (1980) *Social Darwinism and English Thought*, Brighton: Harvester Press.

Jordan, B., James, S., Kay, H. and Redley, M. (1992) *Trapped in Poverty*, London: Routledge.

Joshi, H. (1984) *Women's Participation in Paid Work: Further Analysis of the Women and Employment Survey*, London: Department of Employment.

Kasarda, J.D. (1980) 'The implications of contemporary redistribution trends for national urban policy', *Social Science Quarterly*, 61: 373–400.

—— (1985) 'Urban change and minority opportunities', in P. Peterson (ed.), *The New Urban Reality*, Washington DC: Brookings Institute.

—— (1986) 'The regional and urban redistribution of people and jobs in the US', paper for the National Research Council on National Urban Policy, National Academy of Sciences.

—— (1989) 'Urban industrial transition and the underclass', *Annals of the American Academy of the Political and Social Sciences*, 501: 26–47.

Katz, M.B. (1986) *In the Shadow of the Poorhouse*, New York: Basic Books.

—— (1989) *The Undeserving Poor*, New York: Pantheon Books.

Kay, D. and Miles, R. (1992) *Refugees or Migrant Workers*, London: Routledge.

Keating, P. (1976) *Into Unknown England*, Manchester: Manchester University Press.

Kevles, D.J. (1985) *In the Name of Eugenics*, New York: Alfred A. Knopf.

Kincaid, J.C. (1973) *Poverty and Equality in Britain*, Harmondsworth: Penguin.

Land, H. (1980) 'The family wage', *Feminist Review*, 6: 55–77.

Lane, R. (1985) *The Roots of Violence in Black Philadelphia*, Cambridge, Mass.: Harvard University Press.

Lankester, E.R. (1880) *Degeneration. A Chapter in Darwinism*, London.

Lewis, O. (1968a) 'The culture of poverty', in D.P. Moynihan (ed.), *Understanding Poverty*, New York: Basic Books.

—— (1968b) *A Study of Slum Culture*, New York: Random House.

Lidbetter, E.J. (1933) *Heredity and the Social Problem Group*, London: Edward Arnold.

Liebow, E. (1967) *Tally's Corner*, London: Routledge & Kegan Paul.

Lister, R. (1989) *The Female Citizen*, Eleanor Rathbone Memorial Lecture, Liverpool: Liverpool University Press.

Llewellyn-Smith, H. (1910) 'Economic security and unemployment insurance', *Economic Journal*: 507.

Lockhart, C. (1989) *Gaining Ground*, Berkeley: University of California Press.

Longstaffe, G.A. (1893) 'Rural depopulation', *Journal of the Royal Statistical Society*, 56.

Lowell, J.S. (1884) *Public Relief and Private Charity*, New York: Putnams.

Lurie, I. (1968) *An Economic Evaluation of AFDC*, Washington DC: Department of Labor.

MacGregor, S. (1981) *The Politics of Poverty*, London: Longman.

Mack, J. and Lansley, S. (1984) *Poor Britain*, London: Allen & Unwin.

McLanahan, S. and Garfinkel, I. (1989) 'Single mothers, the underclass and social policy', *Annals of the American Academy of Political and Social Science*, 501, January: 92–104.

McLaughlin, E., Millar, J. and Cooke, K. (1989) *Work and Welfare Benefits*, Aldershot: Avebury.

Macnicol, J. (1987) 'In pursuit of the Underclass', *Journal of Social Policy*, 16: 293–318.

Malthus, T.R. (1989) *An Essay on the Principle of Population* (1806), Vol. 2, ed. P. James, Cambridge: Cambridge University Press.

Mann, K. (1986) 'The making of a claiming class', *Critical Social Policy*, 15: 62–74.

—— (1992) *The Making of an English Underclass*, Milton Keynes: Open University Press.

Marsh, C. (1990) 'The road to recovery', *Work Employment and Society*, 4: 31–58.

Marshall, T.H. (1950) *Citizenship and Social Class*, Cambridge: Cambridge University Press.

Martin, J. and Roberts, C. (1984) *Women and Employment*, London: HMSO.

Marx, K. (1930) *Capital*, Vol. 2, London: J.M. Dent.

Marx, K. and Engels, F. (1953) *Karl Marx and Frederick Engels, Selected Works*, Vol. 1 London: Lawrence & Wishart.

Marx, K. and Engels, F. (1985) [1848] *The Communist Manifesto*, London: Penguin.

Mayhew, H. (1861) *London Labour and the London Poor*, London.

Mead, L.M. (1986) *Beyond Entitlement*, New York: Free Press.

Mearns, A. (1976) *The Bitter Cry of Outcast London* (1883), in Keating (1976), 91–111.

Micklewright, J. (1986) *Unemployment and Incentives to Work: Policy Evidence in the 1980s*, Discussion Paper 92, ESRC Programme on Taxation Incentives and the Distribution of Income, London: London School of Economics.

Moon, J.D. (1988) 'The moral basis of the democratic welfare state', in A. Gutmann (ed.) *Democracy and the Welfare State*, Princeton, NJ: Princeton University Press, 27–52.

Moore, J. (1989) 'The end of the line for poverty', speech to Greater London Area CPC, 11 May.

Moore, R. (1977) 'Migrants and the class structure of Western Europe', in R. Scase, *Industrial Society: Class, Cleavage and Control*, London: Allen & Unwin.

Moran, K. (1985) 'Preface to a feminist theory of poverty', in C. Carson and M. McLeod (eds), *Poverty with a Human Face*, San Francisco: Public Media Centre.

Morel, B.A. (1857) *Traité des dégénérescences physiques, intellectuelles et morales de l'espèce humaine*, Paris.

Morris, L.D. (1984) 'Redundancy and patterns of household finance', *Sociological Review*, 32: 492–522.

—— (1985) 'Renegotiation of the domestic division of labour', in B. Roberts, R. Finnegan and D. Gallie, *New Approaches to Economic Life*, Manchester: Manchester University Press.

—— (1987) 'Constraints on gender', *Work Employment and Society*, 1, 85–106.

—— (1990) *The Workings of the Household*, Cambridge: Polity Press.

—— (1991) *Social Security Provision for the Unemployed*, London: HMSO.

—— (1992) 'The social segregation of the long term unemployed', *Sociological Review*, 38: 344–69.

Morris, L.D. and Irwin, S. (1992) 'Employment histories and the concept of the underclass', *Sociology*, 26: 401–20.

Moylan, S., Millar, J. and Davies, B. (1984) *For Richer For Poorer: DHSS Cohort Study of Unemployed Men*, London: HMSO.

Moynihan, D.P. (1965) *The Negro Family: The Case for National Action*, Washington DC: Office of Policy Planning and Research, US Department of Labor.

Mudge, G.P. (1909) 'Biological iconoclasm, Mendelian inheritance and human society', *Mendel Journal*, 1: 45–124.

Murray, C. (1984) *Losing Ground*, New York: Basic Books.

Murray, C. (1990) *The Emerging British Underclass*, Choice in Welfare Series No. 2., London: Health and Welfare Unit, Institute of Economic Affairs.

Nanton, P. (1991) 'National frameworks and the implementation of local policies', *Policy and Politics*, 19: 191–7.

Neckerman, K., Aponte, R. and Wilson, W.J. (1988) 'Family structure, black unemployment and American social policy', in M. Weir, A.S. Orloff and T. Skocpol (eds), *The Politics of Social Policy in the United States*, Princeton: Princeton University Press, 397–420.

Novak, M. (1987) *The New Consensus on Family and Welfare*, Washington: American Enterprise Institute.

Ogus, A.I. and Barendt, E.M. (1988) *The Law of Social Security*, London: Butterworths.

Pahl, R.E. (1980) 'Employment, work and the domestic division of labour', *International Journal of Urban and Regional Research*, 4: 1–20.

—— (1984) *Divisions of Labour*, Oxford: Basil Blackwell.

Pascall, G. (1986) *Social Policy: A Feminist Analysis*, London: Tavistock.

Patemen, C. (1989) *The Disorder of Women*, Cambridge: Polity Press.

Pick, D. (1989) *Faces of Degeneration*, Cambridge: Cambridge University Press.

Pitt-Rivers, A. (1906) *The Evolution of Culture and Other Essays*, Oxford: Clarendon Press.

Piven, F.F. and Cloward, R.A. (1971) *Regulating the Poor*, New York: Pantheon Books.

Poovey, M. (1989) *Uneven Developments*, London: Virago.

Quincy, J. (1971) 'Report of the Committee on the Pauper Laws of this Commonwealth' (1821), in D.J. Rothman, *The Almshouse Experience: Collected Reports*, New York: Arno Press.

Ray, L.J. (1983) 'Eugenics, mental deficiency and Fabian socialism between the wars', *Oxford Review of Education*, 9: 213–22.

Report of the Mental Deficiency Committee, Part I, Part III (1929), London: HMSO.

Report to the Moreland Commission (1962) New York: Greenleigh Associates.

Rex, J. and Moore, R. (1967) *Race, Community and Conflict*, London: Oxford University Press.

Rex, J. and Tomlinson, S. (1979) *Colonial Immigrants in a British City*, London: Routledge & Kegan Paul.

Ritchie, D.G. (1889) *Darwinism and Politics*, London: Swan Sonnenschein.

Ritchie, J. (1989) *Thirty Families*, London: HMSO.

Ritchie, J. and Faulkner, A. (1989) *Voluntary Unemployment*, London: SCPR.

Roche, M. (1992) *Rethinking Citizenship*, Cambridge: Polity Press.

Rodgers, H.R. Jr (1986) *Poor Women, Poor Families*, New York: M.E. Sharpe.

Rogers, A. (1992) 'New immigration and urban ethnicity in the US', in M. Cross (ed.), *Ethnic Minorities and Industrial Change in Europe and North America*, Cambridge: Cambridge University Press, 226–49.

Rowntree, B.S. (1901) *Poverty. A Study of Town Life*, London: Macmillan.

—— (1941) *Poverty and Progress*, London.

Royal Commission on Unemployment Insurance (1932) *Final Report*, London: HMSO.

Runciman, G. (1990) 'How many classes are there in British society?', *Sociology*, 24: 378–96.

Rutter, M. and Madge, N. (1976) *Cycles of Disadvantage*, London: Heinemann.

SBC: *see* Supplementary Benefits Commission.

Searle, G.R. (1976) *Science in History No. 3*, Leyden: Noordhoff International Publishing.

Shaw, C. (1987) 'Eliminating the yahoo; eugenics, social Darwinism and five Fabians', *History of Political Thought*, 8: 521–44.

Silverman, M. (1992) *Deconstructing the Nation*, London: Routledge.

Simon, J.L. (1989) *The Economic Consequences of Migration*, Oxford: Basil Blackwell.

Sims, G.R. (1883) 'How the poor live', in Keating (1976).

Sinfield, A. (1978) 'Analyses in the social division of welfare', *Journal of Social Policy*, 7: 129–56.

Skocpol, T. (1988) 'The limits of the New Deal System and the roots of contemporary welfare dilemmas', in M. Weir, A.S. Orloff and T. Skocpol (eds), *The Politics of Social Policy in the United States*, Princeton, NJ: Princeton University Press, 293–312.

Smith, D.J. (ed.) (1992) *Understanding the Underclass*, London: Policy Studies Institute.

Smith Rosenberg, C. (1971) *Religion and the Rise of the American City*, Ithaca, NY: Cornell University Press.

Social Trends (1986) London: HMSO.

Stack, C. (1974) *All Our Kin*, New York: Harpers.

tedman-Jones, G. (1984) *Outcast London* (1971), London: Penguin Books.

Stevenson, E.F. (1934) *Unemployment Relief: the Basic Problem*.

Straubhaar, T. (1988) 'International labour migration within a common market', *Journal of Common Market Studies*, 1: 45–60.

Supplementary Benefits Commission (1977) *Low Incomes: Evidence to the Royal Commission on the Distribution of Income and Wealth*, London: DHSS/HMSO.

—— (1979) *Response of SBC to 'Social Assistance': a Review of the Supplementary Benefits Scheme in Great Britain*, London: HMSO.

Taylor-Gooby, P. (1986) 'Citizenship and welfare', in R. Jowell, S. Witherspoon and L. Brook (eds), *British Social Attitudes*, Aldershot: Gower, 1–28.

Titmus, R. (1950) *Problems of Social Policy*, London: HMSO.

—— (1958) 'The social division of welfare', in *Essays on Welfare*, London: Allen & Unwin.

Townsend, P. (1979) *Poverty*, Harmondsworth: Penguin.

Townsend, P. and Gordon, D. (1989) 'What is enough?', paper for International Social Security Conference, Edinburgh, July.

Trattner, W.I. (1974) *From Poor Law to Welfare State*, New York: Free Press.

Vincent, C. (1991) *Poor Citizens*, Harlow: Longman.

Wacquant, L.J.D. and Wilson, W.J. (1989) 'The costs of racial and class exclusion in the inner city', in *Annals of the American Academy of Political and Social Science*, 501 (January): 8–25.

Walker, A. (1990) 'Blaming the victims', in Murray (1990).

Walker, C. (1983) *Changing Social Policy*, Occasional Papers on Social Administration 70, London: National Council for Voluntary Organizations.

Weale, A. *et al.* (1984) *Lone Mothers, Paid Work and Social Security*, London: Bedford Square Press/NCVO.

Webb, S. (1896) *The Difficulties of Individualism*, Fabian Society Tract 69, London: Fabian Society.

—— (1901) *Twentieth Century Politics; a Politics of National Efficiency*, Fabian Society Tract 108, London: Fabian Society.

—— (1907) *The Decline of the Birth Rate*, Fabian Tract 131, London: Fabian Society.

Wilson, W.J. (1978) *The Declining Significance of Race*, Chicago: University of Chicago Press.

—— (1987) *The Truly Disadvantaged*, Chicago: University of Chicago Press.

—— (1991) 'Studying inner-city dislocations', *American Sociological Review*, 56: 1–14.

Yates Report (1971) 'Report of the secretary of state (of New York) in 1824 on the relief and settlement of the poor', in D.J. Rothman (ed.), *The Jacksonians on the Poor*, New York: Arno Press.

Yuval-Davis, N. (1990) 'Women, the state and ethnic processes', paper presented at the Racism and Migration in Europe conference, Hamburg.

Index